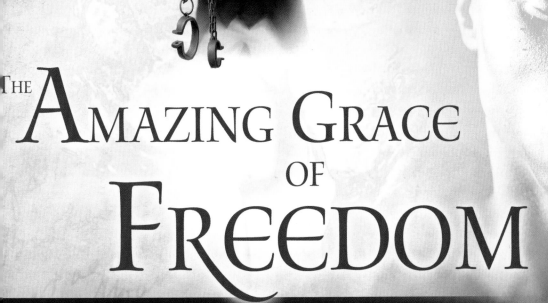

"Wilberforce had
changed the course
of Western civilization,
this great man had
brought the slave
trade to an end...."

– Charles Colson

THE AMAZING GRACE OF FREEDOM

The Inspiring Faith of William Wilberforce

the Slaves' Champion

First Printing: January 2007

ISBN-13: 978-0-89221-673-4
ISBN-10:   0-89221-673-5
Library of Congress Catalog Number: 2006937538

All Scripture is from the New King James Version of the Bible, unless otherwise noted.

Cover and interior design by Brent Spurlock

Printed in the United States of America

For information regarding author interviews, please contact the publicity department at (870) 438-5288.

Please visit our website for other great titles:
www.newleafpress.net

New Leaf Press
A Division of New Leaf Publishing Group

Freedom

Dedication

With the authors' love and great thanksgiving to our Lord and Savior Jesus Christ.
With deepest gratitude and appreciation,
this book is dedicated to Ken Curtis, a noble Christian historian and scholar of history,
whose insight and assistance made the book possible.

Dr. Ted Baehr — to Lili, Peirce, Jim, Robby, and Evy.
Susan and Ken Wales — to Megan, J.B., and Hailey Elizabeth Brown,
and to the memory of Susan's English ancestor, Sir Henry Bedingfield.

Acknowledgments

With deepest gratitude and appreciation to
Tim Dudley and to his exceptional staff at New Leaf Publishing Group,
especially our editor Jim Fletcher, art director Brent Spurlock,
and publicist Laura Welch, and to all the wonderful contributors
and friends of the project.

Contents

Part IV: An Inspiring Look At the Influence of William Wilberforce on Lives and Ministries Today.................................114

Foreword

This book is a gathering of fine writings and thoughts that not only introduces us to William Wilberforce but also delightfully and fascinatingly tells us the struggles, detours, defeats, and ultimate victories in the life of this persevering statesman of man's political domain and faithful, dedicated servant of God in His earthly realm.

Here in these pages you will meet a wonderful friend whose very humanness keeps us close. His transparent openness reveals to us extraordinary qualities that enable his remarkable achievements. He simply and truly *is* one of a kind!

For a filmmaker, the story of Wilberforce is simply irresistible. The beginnings, the changes, the "ups" and the "downs," are the "stuff" of marvelous film stories. Of course, the sudden and marked changes and "reversals of fortune" heighten the drama and ultimately lead to a satisfying resolution and final victory.

And life in our world is better because of the character, determination, perseverance, and sacrifice of this heroic servant of God. The ending is truly redemptive.

This miracle, with God's grace, has happened!

Scenes from the film give us a glimpse of the fascinating story. The telling by superbly talented filmmakers and artisans who crafted this extraordinary film based on the life and times of William Wilberforce is exquisite.

Later, I'll share tales from the making of the film.

William Wilberforce had two great obsessions that involved his total being. The first was the abolition of the slave trade and the other was the reform of manners, morals, and decency, as well as a return to civility in society.

As we travel the path, meeting John Newton and William Wilberforce, you will be amazed, enlightened, and inspired by this incredible story of God at work in the lives of His people on earth.

History has always ultimately shown that God's plans are indeed the best.

We begin our odyssey by hearing John Newton shortly after July 21, 1796, as he writes to William Wilberforce, encouraging him to stay the course and remain in Parliament, so that he may not simply choose between serving God and the world of politics, but that he indeed may do both and in so doing truly change the world.

> [I]f after taking the proper steps to secure your continuance in Parliament, you had been excluded, it would not have greatly grieved you. You would have . . . considered it as a providential intimation that the Lord had no farther occasion for you there. And in this view, I think you would have received your *quietus* [dismissal] with thankfulness. [But] I hope it is a token for good that He has not yet dismissed you.
>
> Some of [God's] people may be emphatically said not to live to themselves. May it not be said of you? . . . You meet with many things which weary and disgust you, . . . but then they are inseparably connected with your path of duty; and though you cannot do all the good you wish for, some good is done. . . .
>
> It costs you something . . . and exposes you to many impertinences from which you would gladly be

FOREWORD BY PRODUCER KEN WALES

Amazing Grace

Rev. John Newton — Wm. Walker

1. A - maz-ing grace, how sweet the sound, That saved a wretch like me!

exempted; but if, upon the whole, you are thereby instrumental in promoting the cause of God and the public good, you will have no reason [for] regret. . . .

Nor is it possible at present to calculate all the advantages that may result from your having a seat in the House at such a time as this. The example, and even the presence of a consistent character, may have a powerful, though unobserved, effect upon others. You are not only a representative for Yorkshire, you have the far greater honour of being a representative for the Lord, in a place where many know Him not, and an opportunity of showing them what are the genuine fruits of that religion which you are known to profess.

Though you have not, as yet, fully succeeded in your persevering endeavours to abolish the slave trade, the business is still in [process]; and since you took it in hand, the condition of the slaves in our islands, has undoubtedly been already [improved]. . . . These instances, to which others . . . might . . . be added, are proofs that you have not laboured in vain.

It is true that you live in the midst of difficulties and snares, and you need a double guard of watchfulness and prayer. But since you know both your need of help, and where to look for it, I may say to you as Darius to Daniel, "Thy God whom thou servest continually is able to preserve and deliver you." Daniel, likewise, was a public man, and in critical circumstances; but he trusted in the Lord; was faithful in his department, and therefore though he had enemies, they could not prevail against him.

Indeed the great point for our comfort in life is to have a well-grounded persuasion that we are, where, all things considered, we ought to be. Then it is no great matter whether we are in public or in private life, in a city or a village, in a palace or a cottage. The promise, "My grace is sufficient for thee," is necessary to support us in the smoothest scenes, and is equally able to support us in the most difficult. Happy the man who has a deep impression of our Lord's words, "Without Me you can do nothing." . . . May the Lord bless you . . . may He be your sun and your shield, and fill you with all joy and peace in believing.[1]

– John Newton

What beautiful thoughts and writing from John Newton, whose early life was so full of turmoil, wrongdoing, and godlessness that he indeed referred to himself as a "wretch" — as we so clearly hear in the words he wrote for the hymn "Amazing Grace," the world's best-known song.

This rich story of Newton's journey from terrible wrongdoing, through his dramatic conversion and in his ceaseless service as a pastor, remains unique in the annals of history. And even more, it has inspired countless souls to turn from their lives of despair to God, Who rescues them and sets them upon a path of newfound faithfulness. In all our lives, we can be constantly recalling this unique story and see a new hope that with God, our lives will indeed be ones that God has saved.

So now, the man, Wilberforce, looms before us. Let us move past merely opening a book with words on pages, and enter into the full-color adventure of this courageous reformer, William Wilberforce, a man needed in his time and a man truly *necessary* for our times.

[1.] Robert Isaac and Samuel Wilberforce, *The Life of William Wilberforce*, 5 vols. (London: John Murray, 1840) Vol. 1 pp. 130-134.

Understanding the Importance of the Movie *Amazing Grace*

The Incredible Talent behind *Amazing Grace*
and How the Movie Can Impact Today's Culture.

Wilberforce (portrayed by Ioan Gruffudd) is pictured aboard the slave ship Madagascar in the English port, surveying with dismay the shackles that were used to tie the hundreds of slaves to the dark decks of the slave ships for their almost endless, despairing journeys. Wilberforce invited members of Parliament and their wives to a seemingly pleasant outing in the harbor and then surprised them with the presence and stench of the actual slave ships.

...sinner and Christ is a great Savior. — JOHN NEWTON

Throughout my career, I have considered the opportunity to make a film a great privilege. Creating a movie affords the filmmaker an incredible platform on which to tell a story as well as a great responsibility — making the right choice of a story to tell. First of all, a filmmaker should choose a tale that entertains. The definition of entertainment is from an early Greek source: entertainment — to *inform with delight*. How extraordinarily appropriate is this fine definition! Of equal importance is choosing a story that has the potential to inspire, transform, or redeem the lives of the audience.

When speaking to aspiring young producers, directors, writers, and actors about the opportunities in the entertainment industry, or teaching production classes at my alma mater, the University of Southern California (USC), I have always impressed upon them the importance of these choices. Many of my students and mentorees have made the right choices, and it is very rewarding to see their excellent work on the screen.

It is a great challenge to serve my Lord and Savior, Jesus Christ, in my life's work. I hope that the motion picture *Amazing Grace* will inspire its viewers to change the world just as its protagonist William Wilberforce was empowered by God to make the world a better place by passing a bill that abolished the slave trade and enabled a reform in society of manners, morals, decency, and a return to civility.

Ken Wales

During the making of the film, I was stunned to discover that 27 million people in the world are victims of slavery today! The public must become aware of the shocking slave trade that still exists. It is my hope that the film *Amazing Grace* will inspire the audience to stand up and demand that something be done for these victims of human trafficking and slavery in our society.

Making a Movie

I have been in the film business for almost 50 years, and it is truly astounding to me that any film ever gets made! Making a movie is a long and arduous process . . . the early stages are precarious at best.

The first step in the production of a film is — choosing the RIGHT story to tell. The myriad ideas, plans, concepts, and dreams must all mesh into the project. A producer must possess a vision coupled with a deep passion for the story . . . sometimes to the point of total obsession. Despite the many obstacles along the way, he or she must be driven to tell the story . . . and believe that the story *must* be told!

The key role of the producer is to be a *shepherd* or guide for the film. He must develop a point of interest so that a company or studio will provide the funding for the production. All this must be done with a keen eye and foresight to determine who the audience will be for the picture, and what company might distribute the film to the theaters. There are many facets that the producer has to deal with before beginning a film . . . its marketability, its capacity for making a profit, its appeal to the audience, and its suitability for distribution.

A filmmaker must never forget that while making a movie is a creative enterprise, it is also a business. All the producer's choices, plans, and decisions must, to the financial decision-makers, make *sense to make cents* . . . or dollars . . . more likely millions, or even billions of dollars!

Hours of time, thought, and research must be put into the production, and attention must be given to every detail. The producer's vision does not always line up with the economics of

Bamport Photography

This picture is from the 15th annual Heartland Film Festival, where Amazing Grace *was the opening night gala presentation and won the "Truly Moving Picture" Award. (L– R) Jeff Sparks, President and CEO of the Heartland Film Festival; Michael Apted, Director,* Amazing Grace, *Sharon Swart, senior editor,* Variety Magazine; *Ken Wales, Producer,* Amazing Grace, *Cary Granat, CEO Walden Media.*

moviemaking. And keep in mind that no producer ever sets out to make a bad movie — but it does happen!

There were many moments during the course of *Amazing Grace* when I felt discouraged, but I never wavered in my trust in God that the story of William Wilberforce would become a reality.

On a humorous note, after my wife Susan saw the first screening of *Amazing Grace*, she speculated, "Ken, no wonder you wanted to do this movie . . . you are so like William Wilberforce!" I can't even begin to compare to the great man, but she was referring to my perseverance on the films that I feel God has called me to do.

Help from Friends

Renowned author and theologian Os Guinness was well versed in the extraordinary work and life of Wilberforce and the reformer's concepts. Os is one of the world's truly great thinkers and theologians. He has been a close friend for many years, and he was the first person I contacted when I became a part of the production team. An invaluable consultant and resource to the project, his insights have constantly shed new light on the importance of Wilberforce's faith and mission to change the world.

Early in the film's development process, I also contacted and became friends with William Wilberforce biographer Kevin Belmonte, whose remarkable work on the reformer's life, *Hero for Humanity*, became the "go-to book" for the film's historical reference and "period accuracy."

Twice, I traveled with Belmonte throughout England, visiting many Wilberforce sites, including his beautifully restored birthplace in Hull. In England, Kevin introduced me to Marylynn Rouse, director of the John Newton Historical Project and a key planner for the celebration of the 200th anniversary of the abolition of the slave trade. The story and its characters came alive as Kevin and I traveled with Marylynn and walked in the footsteps of Wilberforce's

"I hope we open people's eyes to an interesting story that not many people will know about, and that, while being entertained, they learn something about the human condition: that principles exist in the world, and that things can be changed."
— Michael Apted, director of the film
Amazing Grace

journey, visiting his haunts, his homes, his schools, his churches, his memorials, and several museums.

Os Guinness and Kevin Belmonte frequently met with the other members of our production team, advising us throughout the making of the film. It was a delight for me to work with Os, Kevin, and Marylynn throughout my research on the film, and we owe a great deal of the film's authenticity and its historical and spiritual accuracy to these three.

My research was not only invaluable to the film, but also meaningful to me as a Christian as I spent many hours on the Clapham Green, south of London, where the Clapham Circle lived, worshiped, and worked. Throughout the years, I had read many articles about the Clapham Circle that described how this small group of abolitionists influenced the society of their day, ultimately changing the world. Visiting the church where they worshiped was a meaningful experience that I shall never forget. The pastor, David Isherwood, is an avid Wilberforce scholar and a great keeper of the Clapham Circle legacy. His gracious welcome and insight provided glimpses of the memorable events in the life of William Wilberforce.

The Film

To cover 30 years of history in less than two hours was a major challenge of creating the film. The producers, the screenwriter, and the director collaborated on what portion of the life of Wilberforce to depict, and then decided the most efficient way to tell the story, and I believe we were successful considering the amount of material

In this pivotal scene, the Clapham Circle is meeting with William Wilberforce (portrayed by Ioan Gruffudd, second from left) to encourage him to remain in Parliament to lead the efforts to effect social reforms in the slave trade. Wilberforce listens intently as Thomas Clarkson (portrayed by Rufus Sewell, standing) demonstrates the cruel use of shackles and other brutal tools used to restrain slaves on the ships. Seated next to Wilberforce is Hannah More (portrayed by Georgie Glen, third from left), the Clapham leader who reminds Wilberforce that "he can accomplish both of his objectives — to remain in Parliament AND serve God at the same time." During future presentations in Parliament, Wilberforce would repeat this strategy to bring the realities of the slave trade to the attention of an often unaware and uncaring audience.

we had to deal with. Many biopics attempt to go "cradle to grave" with regard to the main character, but two hours, the usual film length, is not nearly enough time to do justice to the significant sequences of the film. Also, we had to work closely with historical consultants to ensure the accuracy and authenticity of the events and period. From the director to the costume designers, the hair stylists, and the production designer and his crew, an enormous amount of research was required. It was exciting to see my dream come true with the talented cast and observe the exquisite work by Charles

Wood, the production designer, and Remi Adefarasin, director of photography, all under the direction of the gifted and talented director Michael Apted.

When we filmed the opening scene of Wilberforce stopping his carriage to rescue the beaten horse, the English weather fully cooperated . . . it was severely cold, gloomy, rainy, and foggy, just what the first scene called for. I think one of the more startling scenes in the film involved Toby Jones as the Duke of Clarence. While playing cards with Wilberforce, the Duke requests that his

Ioan Gruffudd and producer Ken Wales, just before shooting the opening sequence of Amazing Grace. Wilberforce stops his carriage while riding through the early morning countryside with Henry Thornton. (Thornton was one of William Wilberforce's closest confidants, and a leading member of the Clapham Circle, a group of Wilberforce's godly, loyal supporters who bolstered his efforts for not only the abolition of slavery, but also for the reform of manners in society and a return to civility.) Wilberforce stops the carriage, and rushes to the place where a farmer is beating his horse mercilessly to the ground. Wilberforce admonishes the man severely and demands he stop beating the horse, reminding the owner to "just let the horse rest a moment and he will return to his good health."

African coach driver substitute as a form of payment. It's a very dramatic moment in the film, a time where a human life is devalued, and it clearly gives the viewer an understanding of Wilberforce's ardent quest.

I did not have the opportunity to tour an actual slave ship, but the very ship that Wilberforce boarded in the film sailed from Cornwall with a Royal Navy escort to Liverpool and Bristol, the two main centers of the slave trade in England. It then sailed through the English Channel and up the River Thames to a mooring in central London as part of the 200th Bicentennial celebration. Other

slave ships in the film that appeared in the distance were created in computer generated imagery (CGI).

The Director

Our creative team compiled a "wish list" of possible directors who might be appropriate to direct a historical film. We focused our search for a British director who was innately familiar with the period as well as the character, William Wilberforce. It was also important that the director have a track record of successful films, and a reputation for being open and collaborative in the development of the story and the script. In the preproduction phase, we talked to several of the candidates on our list, checking each director's availability. Renowned director Michael Apted was at the top of our list and we were thrilled when we learned he was available.

A British director who resides in Los Angeles, Apted is the current president of the Directors Guild of America, of which I am a member. He is also the critically acclaimed director of numerous films, including the Academy Award nominated *Coal Miner's Daughter*, starring Sissy Spacek, who received an Oscar for her role of Loretta Lynn. Other notable films directed by Apted, many of which received multiple Academy nominations and Academy awards, are *Gorillas in the Mist*, starring Sigourney Weaver; *Enigma*, a World War II drama; and *Nell*, which also garnered an Academy Award for Jodie Foster, who played the title role. In 1999, Apted directed *The World Is Not Enough*, starring Pierce Brosnan as James Bond.

His legendary career not only spans feature films, but also television and documentaries, including his award-winning *49 Up* and the three establishing episodes of HBO's mini-series *Rome*.

Apted possessed all the credentials, as well as the qualities, we desired in a director for our film, *Amazing Grace*. What impressed me personally about Apted was his passion for authenticity in historical films. Most importantly, he shared the vision for the film that Walden Media executives, Cary Granat and Micheal Flaherty, and the other members of Walden and the Bristol Bay Production teams had for the film.

Michael Apted's vision was to tell the story as a political thriller and then show how Wilberforce and his close friends, the Clapham Circle, and his political colleagues, including Prime Minister William Pitt, were able to accomplish their impossible goal — passing the bill to end the slave trade in the British Empire in the 18th century.

Apted sums it up best in these words, "I wasn't interested in making a dull biopic. This is a great period in British politics. I wanted to make a film that showed how heroic and relevant politics can be, and that's impossible to do in a contemporary setting now that politics is so discredited. We have to make politics relevant to our lives — we ignore it at our peril. The only way to do this on screen was to make a film about a topic that no one could argue was anything but a great and wonderful thing — the abolition of slavery. Nowadays, we tend to see politics used for self-interest, but Wilberforce and his associates were able to maneuver their way through that self-interest in their opponents and form alliances to help them reach their goal."

The actors were equally pleased with our directorial choice. After filming *Amazing Grace*, Ioan Gruffudd, who plays Wilberforce, praised Apted. "He is one of the best directors I've worked with, well prepared, with confidence in the actors, the script, and the crew. Every day we knew exactly what we were doing and that inspires actors and gives them confidence to do their best work."

Albert Finney, who played John Newton, said that working with Michael Apted was a pleasure. "He is very well organized — everything moves quickly. Often as an actor you are paid to hang about, but there's none of that with Michael."

Michael Gambon, who plays Lord Fox in the movie, praises director Apted: "He's the best film director I've ever worked with. He films at an alarming rate, and he does very few takes because he knows exactly what he wants. He's charming, talented, and positive."

The Screenplay

"If it's not on the page, it's not on the stage," particularly holds true in a period feature film such as *Amazing Grace*. The historical accuracy and solid content was critical to the success of this project. Without a great script, it is impossible to produce a successful film, attract a good director, or assemble a talented cast. Often, numerous scripts are written before one is agreed upon. The *three* most important elements in the making of a motion picture are — *story, story, story!*

The Screenwriter

Once Apted was hired to direct the film, he suggested we consider British screenwriter Steven Knight, who had recently received an Academy Award nomination for his poignant screenplay, *Dirty Pretty Things.* This critically acclaimed film depicted the heartrending dilemma of illegal immigrants in London, who were forced to sell their body organs on the black market in an effort to survive. Ironically, Apted had a meeting scheduled with Knight for the following day. Again, God's providence! He explained that they had mutual admiration for each other's work, and were hoping to find a project that they could work on together.

After several conferences with Apted and the creative team, Knight reviewed the salient points of his creative process, and then presented his vision for the film: "When I'm writing an original screenplay, I usually think of a scene and see where that leads me, but with a commissioned script based on actual events, the plot is already there; you know what is going to happen. So I decided to find the protagonist, Wilberforce, at his lowest ebb and see how he deals with it. His struggle took place over many years — he devoted 20 years to the Bill, bringing it back to Parliament over and over again. Europe and America were in turmoil, so we had to find a way to get from the beginning of his story to the end without turning it into a history lesson and without using the characters' dialogue to explain it all. Certain events had to be telescoped by finding a key scene and watching how Wilberforce reacts to what is going on."

"I'd like the film to show that standing up for your rights takes courage and will reap rewards in the long run."
– Ioan Gruffudd

The screenwriter ultimately defined the film story by depicting the drama of Wilberforce's 20-year journey through the years of his "ups and downs" in his Parliament battles, finally culminating in a vote by the House of Commons that gave him a resounding victory that ended the slave trade throughout the British Empire. The writer focused on the man, who was instrumental in ending the horrors of the slave trade, and how he was called and empowered by God!

Knight also explained that his research gave him many interesting details that he used in the film to depict Wilberforce's everyday life. "Wilberforce was a single-minded man who kept pursuing his goal and plucked success from the jaws of defeat. To most people at the time, the idea of abolishing the slave trade was ludicrous — like someone today suggesting that we abandon the internal combustion engine right now! At the same time, he was an eccentric. He had a house full of sick animals and could never bring himself to fire any of his staff, so that by the time he was 50, he had a house full of old servants, most of whom did nothing. And he would come home to find his house full of people he didn't know sleeping there."

Casting Wilberforce

After the director is hired and the screenplay is written, the casting process begins. In this process, all the producers and executives presented their "wish list" of actors for the role of William Wilberforce. We approached a few actors, but when our exceptional casting director, Nina Gold, suggested that Welsh actor Ioan Gruffudd (pronounced Yo-an Griff–ith) play the role, the decision to hire him was unanimous! Gruffudd, who had trained at the

The Amazing Grace of Freedom

William Wilberforce (portrayed by Ioan Gruffudd). Wilberforce, in the House of Commons, presents the very long petition with thousands of signatures demanding an end to the vicious slave trade that was supplying the usual commerce. Ioan gives a virtuoso performance.

Royal Academy of Arts in London, possessed all the characteristics needed to play Wilberforce, and was hired immediately.

I had first become acquainted with Ioan when he appeared in the role of Admiral Horatio Hornblower in the PBS series *Hornblower*. He was outstanding in this role, and his performance alone proved that he could play Wilberforce with passion and perfection. More recently, he appeared as Mr. Fantastic in the blockbuster Marvel Comics adaptation, *The Fantastic Four*, and through that performance I identified many more qualities that proved to me he was our Wilberforce.

After Gruffudd was cast to play Wilberforce, he explained what had attracted him to this specific role: "It was the combination of the director, the script, and the story," he replied. "It's very rare to find all three of such a high standard in the same project. I was convinced that I could play this role and that I'd be skillfully guided by Michael Apted."

Ioan Gruffudd and Albert Finney, portraying William Wilberforce and John Newton, respectively. In this scene, the repentant former slave captain is confronted by Wilberforce, who begs for his help in making the people aware of the horrors of slavery. Newton, who has renounced his former career, intends to live out his life quietly in a country parish. Wilberforce, however, persuades him to write down his account of slave trading, and this document proves a decisive key in overturning opposition to the efforts of Wilberforce in the House of Commons.

Gruffudd admits he knew a little about William Wilberforce and his place in history, "I was naïve about his many achievements. Reading about his struggle against the world of his time — it was likened to trying to take away the defense budget or ban the use of oil in the UK today."

The actor said he read extensively to prepare for the role of Wilberforce. Explaining how he immersed himself in the period, he said, "I found William Wilberforce to be a likeable man, constantly conflicted between his faith and his work in Parliament, but at his core he was a humanitarian, filled with compassion and courage. At only 5'4", he had a towering presence and an incredible voice."

Ioan's exceptional talent and abilities coupled with his charisma, innate charm, and wit made him a splendid and authentic Wilberforce. He brought the necessary passion to the role, which was no easy task, especially considering how absorbed Wilberforce was in the call that God had for his life. I believe you will find Ioan Gruffudd's performance in the movie is truly passionate and superb.

The Cast

British casting director Nina Gold did an exceptional job in casting the film. First, she presented a list of actors, and in a collaborative effort with the production team, Michael Apted selected the cast for the film. Affirming Nina Gold's fine work, Ioan Gruffudd accurately describes the importance of casting: "It really bolsters up a project when every role is cast so brilliantly."

To everyone's delight, legendary actor **Albert Finney** was cast in the role of John Newton. Finney has amassed a plethora of impressive credits and awards throughout his long, illustrious career, but he is best known today as the curmudgeon lawyer, actor Julia Roberts' boss, in the Academy Award-winning film, *Erin Brockovich*. Finney is absolutely brilliant in *Amazing Grace* as John Newton, the former slave trader turned preacher.

In his own words, he describes his character: "Newton was a sea captain who profited from the slave trade until, aged 45, he suffered a crisis of conscience and left the sea to enter the Church. There he remained and wrote over 200 hymns, including 'Amazing Grace.' Newton was a mentor to Wilberforce, who turned to him at a time of personal conflict. Newton advised Wilberforce to pursue his dream of the abolition of slavery."

In the movie, Newton says in a poignant scene, "There are two things I have learned from my life — that I am a great sinner, and Christ is a great Savior!" Screenwriter Steven Knight extracted this line directly from John Newton's memoirs, but I can't imagine Newton himself saying the words with as much impact as Albert Finney does on the big screen! The moment Albert Finney delivers the lines is a defining pinnacle in my career as a filmmaker. It just doesn't get any better than this!

Michael Gambon, a distinguished veteran of stage, screen, television, plays Lord Fox. Gambon describes his character, "He's an MP and a member of the British aristocracy who initially opposes the abolition of slavery, but then he changes his views and backs Wilberforce."

Gambon shared Gruffudd's enthusiasm over his fellow cast members. "I knew Ioan's work. He's young, intelligent, and handsome, and I enjoy working with him. I've known Albert for over 40 years and have done a couple of plays and a film with him, so it was good to see him on set. I've loved every minute of my time on the film."

Newcomer **Benedict Cumberbatch** relished his role as William Pitt the Younger, Britain's youngest ever prime minister, and said, "It is initially daunting to take on the role of someone with such iconic stature in British history. I was vaguely aware of the history and had seen some portraits and gained some useful insights from a recent biography of Pitt written by William Hague, former leader of the Conservative Party. He invited us to the Houses of Parliament, and it's a potent and powerful place, which gave me an idea of Pitt's passion for politics and how intoxicating it would have been for him. His father was prime minister before him, and it seemed natural to Pitt to channel all his energy into his parliamentary career. In the film, Pitt starts out as prime minister in his twenties and we follow his relationship with Wilberforce to his deathbed, so I wanted to understand the whole stretch of the man's life. He also suffered from ill health and had been told by doctors to drink two to three bottles of port a day, which obviously took a terrible toll on his health and made him an alcoholic. He was incredibly intense and fiercely intelligent but physically awkward, tall and gangly. His body suffered the ravages of a peptic ulcer, which eventually killed him."

Romola Garai plays Barbara Spooner, Wilberforce's wife, whom he married after only a two-week courtship. She explained how the shortage of material on Barbara Ann Spooner presented a challenge for her: "Michael was keen that we had background material on the period, but little is known of Barbara's life before she married William Wilberforce. In those days, women were still regarded as someone's daughter, wife, or mother, rather than noteworthy in their own right. But as soon as she married Wilberforce, she became part of his movement for abolition, and they remained married for 35 years, till Wilberforce's death in 1833." Romola has a rich background in theater and film, and appeared in *Vanity Fair* and Woody Allen's *Matchpoint* and *Scoop*. She has a delightful energy and fabulous range for portraying a variety of film characters.

Actor **Rufus Sewell** describes the character he played, Thomas Clarkson, a contemporary of Wilberforce: "As a student, he won an essay competition on the subject of slavery and became interested in the subject. Then he traveled the length and breadth of the country, canvassing against the slave trade and gathering information. He joined up with Wilberforce and became the *man in the field*. He was a religious man, but hung out with the wrong types because they would give him proof of the iniquities of the trade."

Sewell emphasized the relevance of the story for today's audiences, "People who do good are not necessarily totally clean-cut and wholesome. The abolitionists were a very mixed bunch of individuals. There is good and bad in everyone, so it's worth appealing to the good in people. This is a film about real human beings doing something good."

Favorite Scenes

Ioan Gruffudd describes one of his favorite scenes. "Wilberforce sings 'Amazing Grace' in a gentleman's club in a very aggressive manner to show his peers who he is and what he stands for. It's a very startling image and an arresting moment in the film."

This scene of Wilberforce making a dramatic public confession of faith by standing and singing "Amazing Grace," reminded me of a time when we were filming the CBS series, *Christy*, and Judy Collins, whose version of "Amazing Grace," is a favorite, performed the song on the series. It was a dream of mine to have Judy sing and she appeared as a blind mountain woman, whose character was the cove's "keeper" of their music. This was the last episode we filmed before we wrapped for holidays, and the cast and crew were exhausted and anxious to finish the show, so they could go home for Christmas! The temperatures had dipped to almost freezing in the mountains of Tennessee, just as Catherine Marshall had described in *Christy*, the book that the series was

"William Wilberforce was a man of faith who considered retreating from the world to devote himself to religion. With a very strong moral drive, based on his religious beliefs, Wilberforce moved in the real world and could form alliances with people he didn't totally approve of in order to get closer to his goal. He proved that although he was driven by a divine purpose to rid the world of this iniquitous slave trade, to execute this mission he needed to be strong, worldly, smart, and political. A combination of Christian visionary and skilled politician, his overwhelming tenacity eventually allowed him to reach his goal."
— *Michael Apted, director, Amazing Grace*

Lord Tarleton (portrayed by Ciaran Hinds). In his debate with William Wilberforce, we sense the tension between these lions, so different from each other in this crucial moral question. Wilberforce was determined and spent his entire political life in the pursuit of the abolition of the slave trade. It would be 26 more years before slavery itself ended in the British Empire. Wilberforce died three days after this, his life complete. The bicentennial of this seminal event will be observed in 2007.

based upon. It was not the great day on the set I had envisioned. But as Judy Collins began to sing, the atmosphere suddenly changed! Silence pervaded the room . . . it was almost as if that moment in time was frozen as her beautiful voice and the words of "Amazing Grace" pierced the hearts of the cast, the crew, and our guests. It was as though a supernatural peace fell upon the set. No longer was anyone anxious, tired, or cold . . . I saw tears in the eyes of everyone — all faiths, young and old, adult and child, man and woman. It doesn't matter who you are. Hearing those words penned by John Newton will stir your soul!

A favorite scene of mine in *Amazing Grace* is Albert Finney's declaration as a sinner. Another favorite scene is an exchange between Wilberforce and his butler, played by Jonathan Swift, laced with both humor and truth. When the butler finds Wilberforce rolling around in the grass, his embarrassed master tries to explain that he was praying. "Oh, so you've found God, Sir?" the amused butler asks him. Wilberforce chuckles, "I think it's more like God found me, and I must say, I find it quite inconvenient!" These lines are priceless. Just as Jesus said, "take the narrow gate . . ." but it's rarely convenient, is it? It's usually a struggle, but oh, what peace we find there!

Aspire to Excellence

Jesus Christ calls us to aspire to excellence in every area of our lives — faith, family, friendship, and career. Producing is no exception! In spite of the generic and budgetary differences between film and television production, I think you will find excellence in the CBS series *Christy*, even though the budget was less than that of a feature film. While producing a feature film is far more exacting than producing a television show, the real luxury of film is that it allows the filmmaker much more time to tell the story. A film can take months to make, whereas a television show can be wrapped in a week or two.

Yet film does have it challenges . . . while a TV series has a chance to build an audience to increase its ratings, a film has only a few days at the box office to be successful. Today, DVDs are an additional source of income for film and television. However, it's very important that films like *Amazing Grace* do well immediately at the box office because high revenue convinces the studio executives to produce more inspirational and redemptive movies.

Barbara Spooner (portrayed by Romola Garai). William met her late in life after being introduced by Marianne and Henry Thornton. The Thorntons became "active matchmakers" as they plotted, schemed, and literally pushed the two to spend time together, encouraging them to take long walks in the garden. William and Barbara shared a great delight as they discovered in each other an enormous passion for actively pursuing an end to the slave trade. She became his staunch encourager and was an abolitionist.

Amazing Grace . . . The Film

The day I arrived on location, it was exhilarating to see the dream come alive as I observed the talented cast and crew. Charles Wood, the production designer, Remi Adefarasin, director of photography, Rick Shaine, the film editor and Jenny Beavan, the costume designer, all under the direction of Michael Apted, did exquisite work on the film.

Charles Wood, the production designer, faced many challenges. There are no Parliament buildings from the 18th century existing in London today, so Wood and his team had to recreate the House of Commons so we could accurately depict the debates and meetings. To accurately reconstruct the original Parliament structure, Wood had to locate a building that would accommodate the member benches, which were located on the ground floor, with the additional gallery created by a U-shaped balcony above. Scouting locations throughout the area, he finally located a deserted church south of London that was built in the 18th century. Again, God's providence!

Taking the structure, Wood used a vintage sketch by an artist from the period who had drawn several scenes of the actual Parliament sessions in the House of Commons, to design the interiors. Wood was astounded to discover William Wilberforce standing in debate in one of the drawings! He also identified many of the Members of the Parliament in the sketches who would be portrayed in the film — Lord Fox, Lord Tarleton, the Duke of Clarence, and many others who were prominent in the slave trade debates. What a treasure!

"It seemed that every spring the daffodils came out, every summer the cherries ripened, and every autumn William Wilberforce would present his bill to the house."

– Barbara Spooner

Researching the film, I visited several historical sites, including Wilberforce's home in Hull, but the most memorable of these tours, was my visit to St. Mary Woolnooth, the church in the center of London where John Newton was the pastor. I walked down the aisle and climbed the stairs to the very pulpit where Newton once delivered his Sunday sermons. Standing in that sacred spot, I closed my eyes, imagining him in this church. Suddenly, the front door opened, startling me, and in came the members of the church choir. I watched them file into the pews to begin weekly practice with their director. To my astonishment, the first piece of music they rehearsed was none other than "Amazing Grace"! Tears filled my eyes and I was transported back in time to when John Newton lived. I shall never forget that moving visit!

Why Wilberforce?

William Wilberforce is a man that Abraham Lincoln once said, "every school child in America should know," yet he is virtually unknown in the 21st century. It is a privilege and an honor to be a part of this excellent production team who introduces Wilberforce to the world today. Society owes a great debt and immense gratitude to this courageous man and the work he accomplished in his lifetime. His life serves is an example for what one man can do when called by God . . . *His wonders to perform*. I hope everyone throughout the world will come to know William Wilberforce through this film and that they will be inspired to seek God for His purpose in their own lives. It is my dream that the life of Wilberforce, as depicted in the film *Amazing Grace*, can become a model of faith for women and men so that they will know that God can equip them, just as he did Wilberforce, to do the job that He has called them to do. In Catherine Marshall's book *Christy*, Miss Alice, the Quaker lady who ran the mission where Christy taught school, encouraged the disheartened young teacher when things became too hard for her bear, "If we don't do the work that God has given us to do . . . then who will do it?"

Romance

I am a romantic who believes that every film needs a good love story! Much to my delight, the writer and director depicted Wilberforce's courtship with Barbara Ann Spooner in several scenes of the movie. This romantic encounter brings us into the hearts of the main characters. Costume designer, Jenny Beaven, explained that since little was known about Barbara Spooner, she used fashionable clothes to establish the character's personality. Actor Romola Garai, who played Spooner, reiterated, "Because the subject matter is politics, we could have gone the dowdy route, but we all decided that she was a stylish woman with a strong personality and should wear her clothes accordingly."

Romola Garai is both appealing and charming as Barbara Ann Spooner, and it's delightful to watch the matchmaking attempts of Henry and Marianne Thornton in the film! Before his conversion, Wilberforce was quite a *bon vivant* about town. Following the call on his life, he became so incredibly driven to abolish the slave trade that he no longer had time for a social life, much less a romance. At one point during his career in Parliament, he entertained the idea of

"At the moment he's not well known in our society, but I'm hoping and praying that the movie will change that! I hope that after seeing Amazing Grace *each and every filmgoer will be encouraged to seek God's purpose for their lives so they can go out and change the world just as Wilberforce did in his time!"*
— Ken Wales

a romance with the sister of one of his political cronies, but when he discovered her desires in life were far different from his, he abruptly ended the budding relationship. Wanting no distractions in his work, he became even more absorbed in his goals, but that all changed when his friend Henry Thornton married Wilberforce's childhood friend, Marianne. Observing Henry's love and passion for her, Wilberforce was filled with a sudden longing for a relationship. When he and Barbara Ann Spooner were introduced, they discovered they shared the same passions and goals in life. Two weeks later they were married!

Purpose

There is a special niche for period films as evidenced by the success of the hit film *Pride and Prejudice*. Many other classic films have won Oscars — *A Lion in Winter*, *Chariots of Fire*, and *A Man for All Seasons*. In addition, Mel Gibson's film *The Passion of the Christ* revealed the overwhelming power of an audience of faith! *Amazing Grace* attracts all of these audiences. This adds up to an entertaining film and compelling experience for every audience.

There were very memorable moments throughout the production, but perhaps the most significant was the first day of filming when I realized that this incredible story of a man who truly changed the world and made it a better place, was the culmination of a dream. William Wilberforce, a man of his time, will become a hero of our time.

So, the question is, what will you do with the gifts you've been given? Will you put them in a drawer and pursue a comfortable life? Or will you choose to defy the odds, step out and confront the injustice in the world? Many choose mediocrity because it's easier than reaching for greatness. My prayer is that you will internalize the life of William Wilberforce and make a difference in your world, whoever and wherever you are.

William Pitt the Younger (portrayed by Benedict Cumberbatch). A close friend and ally of William Wilberforce, Pitt was first elected to the House of Commons in 1781 and forged a solid friendship with Wilberforce; two years later, Pitt was elected prime minister at the early age of 24. Cumberbatch magnificently depicts Pitt in his tireless battle to abolish the slave trade in the British Empire.

In William Pitt's final scene in the film he is visited by Wilberforce as he lies dying. Pitt reaches for Wilberforce's hand and says, "I wish I had your faith."

Amazing Grace is a watershed, world-changing movie. There are more and more movies lately that communicate dramatically the good, the true, and the beautiful such as *The Passion of the Christ*, *Luther*, and *The Lion, the Witch and the Wardrobe*. Also, there are many movies being marketed to people of faith and values. Even so, *Amazing Grace* is unique in that it shows that one person can change the world when called and empowered by God.

Amazing Grace is a gorgeous, inspiring movie about a very Christian person: the abolitionist and reformer William Wilberforce. It has deep, soul-stirring Christian references to the sinfulness of people, the salvation of Jesus Christ, and the divinity of Jesus Christ, with frequent renditions of the great hymn "Amazing Grace."

As this book has explained, William Wilberforce led the fight to stop slavery in 18th century England. After a young life of debauchery, William came to Christ at the age of 25. He believed he was called by God to stop the slave trade and reform morals in England.

The movie begins with William talking to his friend, Prime Minister William Pitt, about the need to reform morals and stop slavery, and then flashes back in time to his conversion. It shows how a group of Christians, concerned about the abolition of slavery, were led by Wilberforce and inspired by the repentant ex-slave trader John Newton (who wrote the lyrics to the hymn "Amazing Grace"). Together, they tirelessly work year after year to get the English Parliament to abolish slavery.

The movie is deeply concerned with faithfulness. It shows William's battles with his weak constitution and chronic pain, his struggles with laudanum (a medicinal form of opium), and the fierce opposition he faced in Parliament.

In the midst of his fight for morality and against slavery, William's marriage brings joy and happiness to his life. His wife helps him transcend his problems.

Ioan Gruffudd does a wonderful job as Wilberforce. In fact, the directing and acting in this movie are superb.

Amazing Grace is captivating to watch and inspiring in its Christian content. Since *The Passion of the Christ*, there has not been a movie with such strong Christian testimony. Best of all, the testimony is on the side of freeing the captives, feeding the hungry, taking care of the needy, and having a practical, deep Christianity that involves faith in action. It deserves four stars and commendation. *Amazing Grace* is a great movie and will be an inspiration to all who see it.

Cast Your Vote

Patron sovereignty has traditionally been commended by Hollywood as the right of patrons to determine what they will choose to see or avoid. In our free society, we can again exercise our freedom to influence the entertainment industry to produce moral, uplifting entertainment. Despite their personal preferences favoring sex, violence, and anti-Christian messages, the producers in Hollywood are ultimately concerned about the bottom line — how much money they can make. If Christians support the good and avoid the immoral, our impact will be quickly felt in Hollywood.

The adversary often convinces us that we are powerless — that there is not much left for us to do except complain, escape, or avoid making choices about the media. The truth is that we have great power. We can change the nature of the entertainment by voting with our wallets.

William Wilberforce Disdained the Theater

William Wilberforce was opposed to the theater as a den of iniquity. In the movie *Amazing Grace*, Wilberforce cleanses the theater just as Jesus Christ cleansed the temple by overthrowing the tables of the moneychangers. Here are some of Wilberforce's thoughts on the theater from his book *A Practical View of the Prevailing Religious System of Professed Christians in the Higher and Middle Classes of this Country Contrasted with Real Christianity*:

There has been much argument concerning the lawfulness of theatrical amusements. Let it be sufficient to remark that the controversy would be short indeed if the question were to be tried by this criterion of love to the Supreme Being. If there were any thing of that sensibility for the honor of God, and of that zeal in his service which we show in behalf of our earthly friends, or of our political connections, should we seek our pleasure in that place which the debauchee, inflamed with wine, or bent on the gratification of other licentious appetites, finds most congenial to his state and temper of mind? In that place, from the neighborhood of which (how justly termed a school of morals might hence alone be inferred) decorum, and modesty, and regularity retire, while riot and lewdness are invited to the spot, and invariably select it for their chosen residence! Where the sacred name of God is often profaned! Where sentiments are often heard with delight, and motions and gestures often applauded, which would not be tolerated in private company, but which may far exceed the utmost

Monument showing the persecution of slavery in Zanzibar, South Africa

license allowed in the social circle, without at all transgressing theatrical decorum! Where, when moral principles are inculcated, they are not such as a Christian ought to cherish in his bosom, but such as it must be his daily endeavor to extirpate; not those which Scripture warrants, but those which it condemns as false and spurious, being founded in pride and ambition, and the overvaluation of human favor! Where surely, if a Christian should trust himself at all, it would be requisite for him to prepare himself with a double portion of watchfulness and seriousness of mind, instead of selecting it as the place in which he may throw off his guard, and unbend without danger! The justness of this last remark, and the general tendency of theatrical amusements, is attested by the same well instructed master in the science of human life, to whom we had before occasion to refer. By him, they are recommended as the most efficacious expedient for relaxing, among any people, that "preciseness and austerity of morals," to use his own phrase, which, under the name of holiness, it is the business of Scripture to inculcate and enforce.[1]

William Wilberforce goes on to note in his great book the negative influence of the theater on the actors:

We must here again resort to the topic of theatrical amusements; and recommend their advocates to consider them in connection with the duty of which we have now been exhibiting some of the leading characters. It is an undeniable fact, for the truth of which we may safely appeal to every age and nation, that the situation of the performers is remarkably unfavorable to the maintenance and growth of religious and moral principle, and of course highly dangerous to their eternal interests. Might it not then be fairly asked, how far, in all who confess the truth of this position, it is consistent with the sensibility of Christian benevolence, merely for the entertainment of an idle hour, to encourage the continuance of any of their fellow-creatures in such a way of life, and to take a part in tempting any others to enter into it? How far, considering that, by their own concession, they are employing whatever they spend in this way in sustaining and advancing the cause of vice, and consequently in promoting misery, they are herein bestowing this share of their wealth in a manner agreeable to the intentions of their holy and benevolent Benefactor? How far also they are not in this instance the rather criminal, from there being so many sources of innocent pleasure open to their enjoyment? How far they are acting conformably to that golden principle of doing to others as we would they should do to us? How far they harmonize with the spirit of the apostle's declaration, that he would deny himself for his whole life the most innocent indulgence, nay, what might seem almost an absolute necessary, rather than cause his weak fellow-Christian to offend? Or, lastly, how far they are influenced by the solemn language of our Savior himself; "It needs must be that offences come, but woe to that man by whom the offence cometh; it were better for him that a millstone were hanged about his neck, and that he were cast into the depths of the sea?" The present instance is perhaps another example of our taking greater concern in the temporal than in the spiritual interests of our fellow-creatures. That man would be deemed, and

justly deemed, of an inhuman temper, who in these days were to seek his amusement in the combat of gladiators and prize-fighters; yet Christians appear conscious of no inconsistency in finding their pleasure in spectacles maintained at the risk, at least, if not the ruin of the eternal happiness of those who perform in them![2]

But Even So . . .

Movies, plays, books, and other media are merely tools of entertainment and communication. They may be used for good or ill. The gospel-based Mystery Plays of the Middle Ages led many to know Jesus Christ, as did the more than 120 movies about Jesus Christ since 1897 such as *The Passion of the Christ, Jesus, Ben Hur*, and *King of Kings*.

Just as a hammer may be used to build a church or to hit someone, the theater may be an instrument for good or bad. And we can redeem the theater, the arts, and the movies.

Every studio now has a Christian film division, and several studios are doing major films with strong Christian content. This does not mean that the studios are not still doing bad movies, but it does mean that there are less of the bad, and an increasing number of the good.

As the great bard William Shakespeare noted, the "pen is mightier than the sword." Fast forward 500 years from Shakespeare's time, and we see that the 21st century mass media of entertainment is mightier than the 16th century printed word, though much of the mass media of entertainment starts with the

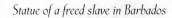

Statue of a freed slave in Barbados

written word. Thus, it is critical that we redeem the values of the mass media of entertainment so that more movies such as *Amazing Grace* are produced and less movies like *Kill Bill*.

More Than Conquerors

Now the adventure begins!

As noted by many theologians, the Word of God sends us into all the world to transform the culture; first, by bringing people to a saving knowledge of Jesus Christ, and then by teaching His disciples through the insightful application of His written Word, the Bible. God sent you on this journey: "Then Jesus came near and said to them, 'All authority has been given to Me in heaven and on earth. Go, therefore, and make disciples of all nations, baptizing them in the name of the Father and of the Son and of the Holy Spirit, teaching them to observe everything I have commanded you. And remember, I am with you always, to the end of the age'" (Matt. 28:18–20; HCSB). And he told you to go to the ends of the earth in Acts 1:8: "But you will receive power when the Holy Spirit has come upon you, and you will be My witnesses in Jerusalem, in all Judea and Samaria, and to the ends of the earth" (HCSB). Not only does He equip you with the power of His Holy Spirit, but He tells you in every single book of the Bible to "fear not" or "do not be afraid" of the adventure He has called you to undertake in His name.

Why does He say, "Fear not"? Because He tells you that you are more than a conqueror: "No, in all these things we are more than conquerors through him who loved us" (Rom. 8:37; NIV). Therefore: "I am persuaded that neither death nor life, nor angels nor rulers, nor things present, nor things to come, nor powers, nor height, nor depth, nor any other created thing will have the power to separate us from the love of God that is in Christ Jesus our Lord!" (Rom. 8:38–39; HCSB).

The same is true for all of us who have accepted Jesus Christ. Jesus suffered on the Cross to win the victory so He could give us the free gift of new life as the adopted sons and daughters of the Creator God who inherit His kingdom.

Thus, as you go into the entire world to redeem the culture, do not be afraid. You are a David against a Goliath, but God has made you more than a conqueror through Jesus Christ. Thus empowered, the Apostles changed the world, and Christians throughout the ages have done the same.

For example, many historians say that the only national charitable act in history was the abolishment of slavery in 1833 in the United Kingdom. Historians note that slavery had been present since the dawn of civilization in every country and that no one in England had an economic incentive to abolish slavery because everyone benefited by it. When William Wilberforce, a young parliamentarian, came to Jesus Christ at the age of 25, God called him to abolish slavery and reform morals in England. In 1791, the first vote to support his bill to stop the slave trade was roundly defeated. Forty-two long years passed before Parliament voted to abolish slavery. William Wilberforce wept as Parliament cheered. When asked why he wept, William Wilberforce said he was a sinful man, but Jesus Christ was a greater God. Subsequently, by God's sovereign grace, William Wilberforce helped instigate the second Great Awakening and the morals in England went from debauched to honorable with people caring for the sick, homeless, and the needy, along with worshiping God in spirit and in truth.

Now, you and your friends and family have a wonderful opportunity to accept God's challenge to go into the entire world to redeem the culture and revive civilization. As you do, remember that all things work for the good for everyone who loves God.

[1] William Wilberforce, *A Practical View of the Prevailing Religious System of Professed Christians in the Higher and Middle Classes of this Country Contrasted with Real Christianity* (London: T. Cadell, jun. & W. Davies, 1797), p. 156–157.

[2] Ibid., p. 161–162.

UNDERSTANDING THE RELEVANCE OF WILLIAM WILBERFORCE

How One Person Plus God Can Make a Difference by Redeeming the Culture: Including the Circumstances & Conditions of His Life & Times

I have a dream that one day "every valley shall be exalted, and every hill and mountain shall be made low, the rough places will be made plain, and the crooked places will be made straight; and the glory of the Lord shall be revealed and all flesh shall see it together."
– Martin Luther King, Jr.

(a Scripture excerpt from his renowned speech, "I Have A Dream")

carried on as this was, must be abolished...

You can change the world. Whether you are 6 or 60, rich or poor, sick or healthy, if you have been called to fight the good fight for truth, justice, faith, and values, you will be more than a conqueror through Jesus Christ who loves you so much.

At universities, colleges, schools, and churches, wherever I teach, preach, or give commencement addresses, young and old come to me burdened by the problems of our world. These concerned individuals want to feed the poor, shelter the homeless, save the unborn, care for the sick, and protect the eyes, hearts, and minds of the innocent, but they feel insufficient and overwhelmed by the problems of society. There is good news for these problems and many more are their opportunities to right wrongs, address needs, and change the world by the power of God's gracious Holy Spirit.

How do I know? Well there are those who went before them who seemed insufficient for the task, but with God's help did the impossible.

One of these Christian reformers who illustrates the power of one plus God in an amazing way was William Wilberforce, who lived from 1759 to 1833. Although William Wilberforce suffered mightily all his life from painfully poor eyesight, serious digestive problems, and a very weak spine, he came to faith, and dedicated himself to (and succeeded in achieving) the abolition of the lucrative slave trade and reforming the morals of a debauched

We are more than conquerors through him who loved us.
– Romans 8:37 (NIV)

society. Thus, William Wilberforce and his small group of dedicated Christian friends, as well as many other saints throughout history, demonstrate not what they could and did do, but what you can and will do empowered by His call and His Spirit.

A World Transformed

England and the British Isles were in a state of moral collapse before William Wilberforce and his associates started to call for an end to slavery and a renewed commitment to Christian faith and values. As Herb Schlossberg points out in Chapter 5, Wilberforce and others transformed a debauched, decadent, unbelieving England by the power of God's grace acting in their lives:

The ignorant became readers, writers, and leaders; the indigent began working and learning to excel at their work; housewives raised their children to be good family people, citizens, and neighbors; paupers and drunks began to earn a living, to save and invest and send their children to the universities and their grandchildren to the House of Commons. An often brutal society in which a woman walking alone on the street could expect to be at least verbally molested, in which the highways were unsafe for the unarmed, in which political corruption was common, in which

INSPIRATION BY DR. TED BAEHR

Glover pastel portrait of Wilberforce

sexual promiscuity was the norm, had by the early years of the new century become kinder, more loving, and — dare we say it? — more Christian. . . .

When Alexis de Tocqueville arrived in the 1830s and observed the contrast that Francis Place was talking about, he concluded that a great revolution had taken place in England and was still in process, but a revolution very different from those of his native France. He was particularly struck by the fact that the nobility of England were fully engaged in the reconstitution of religious and moral living that was taking over the country. . . .

Of course, if that is all that had happened, just a little ceremony superimposed upon the same set of habits and relationships, it would have had little meaning. But Tocqueville observed that the culture had changed in profound ways that were symbolized by such ceremonies, and that is why he called the changes revolutionary. . . . Everywhere Tocqueville traveled in England he saw this sort of devotional exercise, which he knew very well he would not have seen a half-century earlier.

In many ways, the Great Britain of William Wilberforce's day was much like the United States of America and the Western Europe of today. The Western European countries were once filled with the healing salt and saving light of the gospel of Jesus Christ. The dedicated Christians in those countries built hospitals, schools, charities, and sent out missionaries to help those in need throughout the world. As a result of their faith in God, they prospered, and regrettably, all too often, the prosperity God pours out upon His chosen people precedes judgment, as succeeding generations begin to

"I saw her dragged along the aisle."

An example of the kind of cruelty slaves faced

believe a treacherous lie that they themselves created wealth without God.

God has no grandchildren, only children who hear His Word and turn from their self-destructive ways to live in His grace. If future descendants of the civilized people of His kingdom do not hear His good news and instead forget the homeless, the needy, and the weak, and become selfish, indolent, and corrupt and finally forget Him who gave them civilization, they sacrifice their progeny on the altar of Self and eventually stew in the juice of their own sin. As God warned the Israelites:

For the LORD thy God bringeth thee into a good land, a land of brooks of water, of fountains and depths that spring out of valleys and hills; A land of wheat, and barley, and vines, and fig trees, and pomegranates; a land of oil olive, and honey; A land wherein thou shalt eat bread without scarceness, thou shalt not lack any thing in it; a land whose stones are iron, and out of whose hills thou mayest dig brass. When thou hast eaten and art full, then thou shalt bless the LORD thy God for the good land which he hath given thee.

Beware that thou forget not the LORD thy God, in not keeping his commandments, and his judgments, and his statutes, which I command thee this day: Lest when thou hast eaten and art full, and hast built goodly houses, and dwelt therein; And when thy herds and thy flocks multiply, and thy silver and thy gold is multiplied, and all that thou hast is multiplied; Then thine heart be lifted up, and thou forget the LORD thy God, which brought thee forth out of the land of Egypt, from the house of bondage; Who led thee through that great and terrible wilderness, wherein were fiery serpents, and scorpions, and drought, where there was no water; who brought thee forth water out of the rock of flint; Who fed thee in the wilderness with manna, which thy fathers knew not, that he might humble thee, and that he might prove thee, to do thee good at thy latter end; And thou say in thine heart, My power and the might of mine hand hath gotten me this wealth. But thou shalt remember the LORD thy God: for it is he that giveth thee power to get wealth, that he may establish his covenant which he sware unto thy fathers, as it is this day.

– Deuteronomy 8:7–18

As a result of the Church losing its fervor and the prosperous forgetting God's grace, our Western cultures are becoming increasingly decadent and barbaric. We now routinely kill our unborn children, promote perversion and debauchery, encourage the old to die, forget the homeless and the needy, and wallow in the consequences of debauchery such as HIV/AIDS and out of control STDs.

William Wilberforce addressed similar problems in his age head on by confronting the lukewarmness and self-righteousness consuming the English church in his famous book, *A Practical View of the Prevailing Religious System of Professed Christians in the Higher and Middle Classes of This Country Contrasted with Real Christianity*[1]:

BEFORE we consider particular defects in the religious system of the bulk of professed Christians, it may be proper to point out the very inadequate conception which they entertain of the importance of Christianity in general, of its peculiar nature, and superior excellence. If we listen to their conversation, virtue is praised, and vice is censured; piety, perhaps, is applauded, and profaneness condemned. So far is well. But let any one, who would not be deceived by "barren generalities," examine more closely, and he will find, that not to Christianity in particular, but, at best, to religion in general, perhaps to mere morality, their homage is paid. With Christianity, as distinct from these, they are little acquainted: their views of it have been so cursory and superficial, that, far from discerning its characteristic essence, they have little

more than perceived those exterior circumstances which distinguish it from other forms of religion. There are some few facts, and perhaps some leading doctrines and principles, of which they cannot be wholly ignorant; but of the consequences, and relations, and practical uses of these, they have few ideas, or none at all.

View their plan of life and their ordinary conduct; and, not to speak at present of general inattention to things of a religious nature, let us ask, wherein can we discern the points of discrimination between them and professed unbelievers? . . .

Let their conversation take a graver turn: here at length their religion, modest and retired as it is, must be expected to disclose itself; here, however, you will look in vain for the religion of Jesus. Their standard of right and wrong is not the standard of the Gospel: they approve and condemn by a different rule; they advance principles and maintain opinions altogether opposite to the genius and character of Christianity. . . .

Bountiful as is the hand of Providence, its gifts are not so bestowed as to seduce us into indolence, but to rouse us to exertion. . . .

And it may be sufficient here to remark in general, that Christianity is always represented in Scripture as the grand, the unparalleled instance of God's bounty to mankind. It was graciously held forth in the original promise to our first parents; it was predicted by a long continued series of prophets; the subject of their prayers, inquiries, and longing expectations. In a world

> *Britain: "The land of William Wilberforce — who dared to stand up to demand that the slaves in our country should be freed." — Nelson Mandela speaking to Parliament*

which opposed and persecuted them, it was their source of peace, and hope, and consolation. At length it approached —the desire of all nations—a multitude of the heavenly host hailed its introduction, and proclaimed its character; "Glory to God in the highest, on earth peace, good will towards men." It is everywhere represented in Scripture by such figures as may most deeply impress on us a sense of its value. It is spoken of as light from darkness, as release from prison, as deliverance from captivity, as life from death. "Lord, now lettest thou thy servant depart in peace, for mine eyes have seen thy salvation," was the exclamation with which it was welcomed by the pious Simeon; and it was universally received and professed, among the early converts, with thankfulness and joy. At one time, the communication of it is promised as a reward; at another, the loss of it is threatened as a punishment. And, short as is the form of prayer taught us by our blessed Savior, the more general extension of the kingdom of Christ constitutes one of its leading petitions. . . .

This is not the place for inquiring at large, whence it is that those who assent to the position that the Bible is the word of God, and who profess to rest their hopes on the Christian basis, contentedly acquiesce in a state of such lamentable ignorance. But it may not be improper here to touch on two kindred opinions, from which, in the minds of the more thoughtful and serious, this acquiescence appears to derive much secret support. The one is, that *it signifies little what a man believes; look to his practice.* The other, of the same family, that *sincerity is all in all.* Let a man's opinions and conduct be what they may, yet, provided he be sincerely convinced that they are right, however the exigencies of civil society may require him to be dealt with amongst men, in the sight of God he cannot be criminal!

It would detain us too long to set forth the various merits of these favorite positions. The former of them is founded altogether on that grossly fallacious assumption, that a man's opinions will not influence his practice. The latter proceeds on this groundless supposition, that the Supreme Being has not afforded us sufficient means for discriminating truth from falsehood, right from wrong; and it implies, that be a man's opinions or conduct ever so wild and extravagant, we are to presume that they are as much the result of impartial inquiry and honest conviction, as if his sentiments and actions had been strictly conformable to the rules of reason and sobriety. . . . Nay, the absurdity of this principle might be shown to be even greater than what has yet been stated. It would not be going too far to assert, that whilst it scorns to defend petty villains, those who still retain the sense of good and evil, it holds forth a secure asylum to those more finished criminals, who, from long habits of wickedness, are lost alike to the perception and the practice of virtue; and that it selects a seared conscience, and a heart become callous to all moral distinctions, as the special objects of its care. Nor is it only in profane history that instances like these are to be found, of persons committing the greatest crimes with a sincere conviction of the rectitude of their conduct. Scripture will afford us parallels; and it was surely to guard us against this very error that our blessed Savior forewarned his disciples: "The time cometh, that whosoever killeth you will think that he doeth God service."

It is to [the scriptures] we would earnestly call you; to these, ever to be accompanied with fervent prayers for the Divine blessing, Scripture everywhere holds forth the most animating promises. "Ask, and ye shall receive; seek, and ye shall find; knock, and it shall be opened unto you." — "Ho! every one that thirsteth, come ye to the waters." Such are the

The Wilberforce Memorial Column, Hull, as it appeared in the 1800s

when finally summoned to the bar of God, to give an account of our stewardship, what plea can we have to urge in our defense, if we remain willingly and obstinately ignorant of the way which leads to life, with such transcendent means of knowing it, and such urgent motives to its pursuit?

William Wilberforce's voice and the voice of many of his friends and associates were heard. In this book, we will:

- Help you understand the relevance of William Wilberforce and how one person plus God can make a difference in redeeming the culture

- Give you insights into the biography and character of William Wilberforce and into the men and women of faith and values who helped to reform England and the world

- Help you understand the importance of the movie *Amazing Grace* about William Wilberforce and some of the stories of the talent behind the film

- Help you learn about Wilberforce and his impact today on Christian leaders and an inspirational look at how you too can grow in faith, knowledge, and understanding, and so make a difference in the world today.

comfortable assurances, such the gracious encouragements to the truly sincere inquirer. How deep will be our guilt, if we slight all these merciful offers! How many prophets and kings have desired to hear the things that we hear, and have not heard them! Great, indeed, are our opportunities, great also is our responsibility. Let us awaken to a true sense of our situation. We have every consideration to alarm our fears, or to animate our industry. How soon may the brightness of our meridian sun be darkened! Or, should the longsuffering of God still continue to us the mercies which we so much abuse, it will only aggravate our crime, and in the end enhance our punishment. The time of reckoning will at length arrive. And

William Wilberforce's goal was to stop slavery and reform manners, and against all odds he did — but only by the grace of his Sovereign Lord and Savior Jesus Christ. This same Creator God has told you to go on an adventure to bring good news and disciple the nations. So, fear not and go forth to love and serve the Lord by redeeming the time and reforming the culture until it is transformed into a magnificent civilization like a city set on a hill!

[1] *A Practical View of the Prevailing Religious System of Professed Christians in the Higher and Middle Classes of This Country Contrasted with Real Christianity* (London: T. Cadell & W. Davies, 1797), p. 13–24

Facts

- William Wilberforce regarded slavery as a national crime for which all Englishmen were responsible. In 1818 he wrote in his diary, "In the Scripture, no national crime is condemned so frequently and few so strongly as oppression and cruelty, and the not using our best endeavors to deliver our fellow-creatures from them."

- Wilberforce and his friends engaged in an antislavery public opinion campaign unprecedented in English history. In 1814, they gathered one million signatures, one-tenth of the population, on 800 petitions, which they delivered to the House of Commons.

- The English ruling classes viewed abolitionists as radical and dangerous, similar to French revolutionaries of the day.

- Antislavery bills of one sort or another were defeated in Parliament for 11 consecutive years before the act abolishing the slave trade was passed in 1807.

- Slave ship crews were often treated more cruelly than slaves. Slaves brought a profit, so there was incentive to ensure they were adequately fed and cared for. In fact, the death rate for crews was higher than that for slaves.

- Wilberforce was one of five members of the Clapham Sect (the aristocratic circle of Christian activists) who held seats in the House of Commons who never lost a parliamentary election.

- In the summer of 1833, Parliament passed the second reading of the Emancipation Act, ensuring the end of slavery in the British Empire. Three days later, Wilberforce died.

- Evangelical abolitionists have received high praise from secular commentators. For example, 19th-century historian W.E.H. Lecky said, "The unweary, unostentatious, and inglorious crusade of England against slavery may probably be regarded as among the three or four perfectly virtuous pages comprised in the history of nations."

- Slavery wasn't the only social issue that troubled 19th-century British Christians. Between 1780 and 1844 they founded at least 223 national religious, moral, educational, and philanthropic institutions and societies to alleviate child abuse, poverty, illiteracy, and other social ills.

- Among the religious and benevolent societies for impoverished or exploited women were
  - Forlorn Females Fund of Mercy
  - Maritime Female Penitent Refuge for Poor, Degraded Females

LITTLE-KNOWN OR REMARKABLE FACTS ABOUT WILLIAM WILBERFORCE BY RICHARD V. PIERARD

- Society for Returning Young Women to Their Friends in the Country
- Friendly Female Society for the Relief of Poor, Infirm, Aged Widows, and Single Women of Good Character Who Have Seen Better Days

- Books about discouraging social problems became best sellers. For example, in *In Darkest England and the Way Out* (1890), Salvation Army founder William Booth described England's "submerged tenth," trapped in vice, poverty, and godlessness, and explained his plan to end unemployment. The book sold one million copies.

- In their efforts to reform society, many British evangelicals criticized such amusements as dancing, hunting, playing cards, theater going, reading novels, and even Handel's oratorios.

- Some clergy in Victorian Britain gained notoriety for their political activism. Francis Close was called the "Evangelical Pope of Cheltenham" for his attacks on local horse racing. George S. Bull, an evangelical pastor in Yorkshire, was so active in the campaign to reduce children's work hours that he was labeled "The Ten-Hours Parson."

- The evangelical faith and social concern that so permeated 19th-century England led French historian Ely Halevy to say evangelicalism made possible "the extraordinary stability which English society was destined to enjoy throughout a period of revolution and crises."

EDITOR'S NOTE:
Richard Peirard is professor of history at Indiana State University. He co-authored Two Kingdoms: The Church and Culture Throughout The Ages *(Moody, 1993). Reprinted by permission from* Christian History – Issue 53 (Vol. XVI, No1).

Statue of William Wilberforce at St. John's College, Cambridge

The Amazing Grace of Freedom | 39

I t was the most powerful nation on earth, an empire upon which the sun literally never set – not the United States of America in the 21st century, but Great Britain in the 18th and 19th centuries. Because of the wealth pouring into England from her colonies and the Industrial Revolution, many of the destitute rose out of poverty and became members of the middle class. While the rich grew richer, poor working men, women and children toiled sixteen hours a day, six days a week in the drab and dangerous caverns of the newfangled factories. Hopeful country folk immigrated to cities seeking work and found themselves crowded into unsanitary and unsafe dwellings owned by landlords intent on profit over decency. As a result of the overcrowding and a lack of clean water, cholera, typhoid, and tuberculosis plagued thousands of men, women and children. As Mark Galli noted:

> In the early 1800's, Britain was a superpower rolling in wealth. Yet impersonal forces – specifically the Industrial Revolution and the international slave trade – conspired to destroy lives. The masses of England seemed doomed to perpetual poverty, and thousands upon thousands of Africans (and more each year) were locked in perpetual servitude. A lot of Britons looked at their world and then looked for their fishing poles [to escape].
>
> William Wilberforce did not. Neither did Elizabeth Fry or Robert Raikes or Thomas Chalmers, among others – Christians largely forgotten in our day. Yet before the century ended, nearly everything they touched had

Mary Evans Picture Library

Elizabeth Fry frequently visited prisons, even accompanying women to the scaffold to comfort them in their last hours.

improved: prisons, medical care, education, factory conditions, slums. And decades before Americans started shedding uncountable gallons of blood over slavery, the English had simply outlawed it.

The Best of Times, the Worst of Times by Dr. Ted Baehr

If these Christians didn't bring in the kingdom of heaven, they did make England more just. And if they didn't solve every social problem (and certainly, like all successful reformers, they created a few along the way), at least they made life bearable for millions and saved the lives of millions more.

That is no small legacy. And it is a legacy that history shows we hand on to our children, and to our children's children – as long we decided not to trade social compassion for a fly rod.[1]

While economists would contend that life is much better for most Americans today, there are many similarities between Great Britain in the 18th century and the United States. Then as now, the nation's problems could only be solved by transcending entrenched political positions. By believing and applying the whole gospel with a deep faith in Jesus Christ and His written Word, William Wilberforce and his friends tackled problems that today would be divided into conservative and liberal causes: morality on one hand and the abolition of slavery and social justice on the other. Thus, the left (liberal) and the right (conservative) of the political spectrum can both claim William Wilberforce as a role model in part because of the wide range of his influence and because he was not beholden to the political partisanship of his day, but a mere servant of a loving and just God. Although both red state and blue state pundits now extol the achievements of William Wilberforce, during his term in Parliament, he was reviled and applauded by both sides of the aisle.

The miraculous nature of God acting in and through William Wilberforce and his associates to abolish slavery and reform manner is noted eloquently by Howard Temperley in his June 21, 2006, *London Times* review of David Brion Davis's book titled: *Inhuman Bondage: The Rise and Fall of Slavery in the New World.*

An illustration of the poverty that was rampant in the streets of London

From London: A Pilgrimage by Gustave Doré (Dover Publications)

The divide between the rich and the poor was immense in Wilberforce's time.

Indeed, on the basis of the available evidence it would appear that Britain's interests would have been best served by expanding the slave trade and broadening the frontiers of its slave empire. Just as the US expanded its slave system westward along the Gulf Coast into Texas, so Britain could have established new slave regimes in Trinidad, British Guiana and other recently acquired territories. Instead of seeking to suppress the slave trade, it could have dominated it, and in the process out-produced Brazil and Cuba, increased its own wealth, and contributed to the economic growth of the Americas. No wonder Disraeli called abolition "the greatest blunder in the history of the English people."

In his *History of European Morals from Augustus to Charlemagne* (1869), W. E. H. Lecky describes England's crusade against slavery as "among the three or four perfectly virtuous acts recorded in the history of nations." Great powers do not as a rule behave selflessly. Not surprisingly,

Lecky's comment has generally been regarded with scepticism. Now, knowing vastly more than he did about slavery and its abolition, Davis believes Lecky was basically right. Although the American abolition movement came later and assumed a somewhat different character, the same might equally well be said of it. Slaves had never liked being slaves, but the rise of a climate of opinion that objected to slavery on moral grounds was something new. There had been nothing like it in ancient or medieval times or in any other society of which we have record. The upsurge of popular support for abolition both in Britain and the northern USA was unprecedented. Perhaps, David Brion Davis hypothesizes, moral progress is possible.

Whatever lay behind it, the cost of doing away with what up to then had been a resilient, flexible and expanding institution proved formidable. "I thank God," declared Wilberforce on his deathbed, "that I should have lived to witness a day in which England is willing to give twenty millions sterling for the Abolition of slavery." In terms of loss of trade, the cost was much greater. The United States, confronted by a far larger problem and lacking a central government capable of solving it peacefully, barely survived the ordeal.[2]

The miracle of abolition against all odds and all economic interests demonstrates how one person plus God, as the saying goes, can change the world. That person could be you if you allow yourself to be called and empowered by God.

[1] From *Christian History* – Issue 53 (Vol. XVI, No1) P. 6.
[2] Howard Temperley in his June 21, 2006, *London Times* review of David Brion Davis's book titled: *Inhuman Bondage: The Rise and Fall of Slavery in the New World* (Oxford University Press, 2006).

Children presenting a petition for the abolition of the slave trade, from an English children's book (c. 1830)

Historians have identified three Great Awakenings — notable surges of religious vitality — in American history. The first occurred in the second quarter of the 18th century, the second in the opening decades of the 19th century, the third in the period following World War II. The term "Great Awakening" is loose and contested. Critics of the religious revival of the 1950s, for example — the names Peter Berger and Martin Marty come to mind — saw it as largely superficial and lacking in theological bite. Some observers of the current religious scene report glimpses of a Fourth Great Awakening, while others see only a secularist wasteland.

But whether or not current religious movements are powerful enough to make their way into the history books is of less importance than the question of whether they can have much of an effect on the way people actually live in their society. Does a renewal of religious conviction make much difference in the quality of life in a given society? Some of the most disquieting trends in America have taken place just when religious life, by some measures, has flourished. Widespread divorce, sexual antinomianism, rampant crime and bulging prisons, the belief amply demonstrated by polls that there is no such thing as a universal standard of moral behavior, and general boorishness and discourtesy — all coexist and grow along with the flourishing of religious activity. Moreover, some of the statistics show little difference in the indices of social pathology among people with a religious commitment compared to those without one. Is religion irrelevant to behavior, at least on the macro level? If so, is it contingently or necessarily irrelevant? Is it possible for private worship and associated activities to have much effect on the way

society goes about its business? Or must the public square remain forever naked despite the personal convictions of the inhabitants?

Gerhard Lenski, a sociologist of religion who has studied this issue, concludes that it is a mistake to measure the influence of religious associations on society exclusively by their success or failure in bringing about the institutional changes they advocate. He thinks that far more important than those organized campaigns are the "daily actions of thousands (or millions) of group members whose personalities have been influenced by their lifelong exposure" to religious influences. The Cambridge historian Herbert Butterfield once remarked that the importance of Christianity in the history of the West cannot really be understood very well by the historian who draws his information exclusively from documents. It lies rather in the constant preaching to the multitudes — often illiterate multitudes — of love and humility week after week, so that the way people feel, think, and behave is vastly different than it otherwise would have been. Butterfield concluded that this phenomenon has tended "greatly to alter the quality of life and the very texture of human history."

These cultural traits have powerful effects on the direction and force of a society. Who, for example, could calculate the magnitude of the effects of the replacement of *honor* as an ideal by *humility*? A slight that might be taken as sufficient to require a duel can be forgiven by a man who newly thinks such affronts are best met by love. There is also a strong cultural force in *repentance* as a theologically sanctioned and socially accepted requirement because it permits the turning away from destructive behavior to a new beginning. When such acts are multiplied by the millions

---

HOW GREAT AWAKENINGS HAPPEN BY HERBERT SCHLOSSBERG

it cannot help but bring about large-scale change, the sort that the historian can only despair of trying to track and quantify.

Is that just a theory, or can it be substantiated by concrete historical events? As a test case, consider the society that occupied England for most of the 19th century. The stereotypes have become so embedded in our consciousness that the mere utterance of "Victorian" is enough to evoke for most educated people disagreeable images: not only smoky factories and ugly buildings and furnishings, but also a kind of pervasive moral squalor. Contempt drips from the pens of many analysts, both contemporary and modern. H.G. Wells, a product of the late Victorian period, called it "slovenly and wasteful," with its contemptible dwellings, railways, furnishings, art, and literature. Lytton Strachey's *Eminent Victorians* showed the eminences to be ridiculous characters, not to be taken seriously, however seriously *they* seemed to take everything, especially themselves. A recent volume published by the Oxford University Press speaks of the "special place" that the Victorian age has in the present culture. "More than any other era it awakens in us our capacities to feel hostile toward a past way of life, to perceive the past as alien, unenlightened, and silly."

Examples could be multiplied, but they seem to consist of two main complaints: the Victorian age for most of these critics was too capitalist and too religious. The critics focus, often tendentiously,

WILLIAM WILBERFORCE.
ÆT. 29.

Young Wilberforce

on individual biographies and on institutional, aesthetic, and economic issues, less on cultural manifestations — the moral and interpersonal factors that determine the quality of life — that to Lenski and Butterfield were the essences of the thing.

Rather than assessing the Victorian age backwards, try to approach it as it came into being — from the preceding centuries. The restoration of the English monarchy in 1660 brought with it revulsion against the excesses of the Puritan regime that had expired with Oliver Cromwell; but it also ushered in the very different excesses of the court of Charles II. The new king was concerned enough to be rid of Puritan influences that he had Cromwell's body ripped from the grave for public exhibition, but he was even more anxious to rid himself of the bother of having real, live Puritans, and he contrived to have them excluded from the ministry of the Church of England. After the next reign was brought to a hasty conclusion by the Glorious Revolution of 1688, William and Mary evicted from their livings staunch Anglo-Catholic clergymen who could not find it in their conscience to switch allegiances away from the deposed James II. Thus, in the course of a generation, both wings of the Church of England were lost. A historian reports the results:

The "moderate," "reasonable" men, the time–servers, self–seekers, and pluralists — these all were left: but the wings of faith were gone. Had the "National" Church studied how best to extinguish all spiritual fire within the realm and to crush all crusading initiative, she could have devised no better plan than these two tragic expulsions.

The results were not long in coming, and analyses of the Anglican Church from the late 17th through much of the next century were mostly dismal. Perhaps the low point came in the 1730s, when Bishop Butler, in the preface to his famous *Analogy of Religion*, summed up the situation in this way:

> It is come, I know not how, to be taken for granted, by many persons, that Christianity is not so much as a subject of inquiry; but that it is, not at length, discovered to be fictitious. And accordingly they treat it, as if, in the present age, this were an agreed point among all people of discernment; and nothing remained, but to set it up as a principal subject of mirth and ridicule, as it were by way of reprisals, for its having so long interrupted the pleasures of the world.

That was the decade, however, in which John and Charles Wesley discovered what had eluded them until then: the transformative power of real Christian faith as opposed to the nominal adherence that seemed to be the destiny of much of the Georgian era. Out of that came the Methodist "classes" — small groups of believers meeting together for Bible study, discussion, prayer, and mutual encouragement and accountability. Along with the spread of these groups in myriad mining, fishing, and textile towns, scattered Anglican parishes came to life, when clergymen caught the meaning of the gospel in personal ways, experienced the conversion that came to be the hallmark of the evangelical movement, and preached Christian faith centered on the person and work of Jesus Christ.

Meanwhile the dissenting churches, mainly the Baptist and Congregationalist, having descended into a funk similar to that of the Church of England, caught some of the same vision, and by the end of the century were for the most part firmly in the evangelical camp. If the state of technology had permitted it, a moving graphic of the growth of what the period called "experimental religion" would have shown widely dispersed dots appearing early in the century, gradually thickening on the map, until by the end of the century there were influential concentrations of evangelicals all over England. Societies to extend mission and to do good works sprang up all over the nation, and publications at all levels — from tracts intended for near-illiterates to collections of sermons to journals full of historical,

The Clapham Antiquarian Society

Wilberforce was a part of the "Clapham Sect" who effected many changes in their culture.

The Amazing Grace of Freedom

political, and theological reasoning — began appearing, supplemented by newspapers and pamphlets.

A number of politically minded evangelicals under the leadership of William Wilberforce settled in the town of Clapham, south of London, and engaged in highly visible activism. To this group belongs much of the credit for the outlawing of the slave trade in 1807 after two decades of intense labor, and the total abolition of slavery throughout the British Empire in 1833 within a few days of Wilberforce's death — the end of a struggle that had lasted half a century. Among the other projects of the evangelicals was the enactment of factory and mine legislation to mitigate the harshness of life in the enterprises that came out of the industrial revolution, especially for women and children. Charitable work abounded both through societies and by individual initiative. It was also a great age of joyful and abundant giving for myriad good works. Some of the leaders of the Clapham group gave away more than half their incomes.

There were two later movements within the Church of England that broadened the stream of renewed Christianity begun by the evangelicals. At Rugby school the newly appointed headmaster Thomas Arnold determined to break with the brutality and paganism that marked the public schools in order to make the place a training ground for Christian gentlemen. Arnold had been much influenced by the theological and philosophical ideas of Samuel Taylor Coleridge, and both Coleridge and Arnold are usually considered to be early leaders of the Broad Church. But in fact they were very different from the Broad Church figures who appeared on the scene after mid-century, clergymen like Benjamin Jowett of Oxford and Arthur Stanley, Dean of Westminster, whose connections with historic Christian thought seemed tenuous to many critics. Within a few years, even Arnold's adversaries at Oxford were remarking on the serious Christians that were appearing at the universities from Rugby.

At Oxford itself, another group appeared in the early 1830s that called for a renewed appreciation for the historical nature of the Church, looking for inspiration to the theology and traditions of the early Christian centuries. Under the leadership of John Henry Newman and a few colleagues, they issued "tracts" that were actually sophisticated theological documents and called for an end to laxity and to the complacency of a Church willing to be dominated by political leaders, many of whom did not even pretend to be loyal to it. The movement lasted only for about seven years before its miscalculations destroyed its base at Oxford. But the "Tractarian" influence continued for decades in parishes all around England after the Oxford center had withered.

This brief sketch of the main elements of the religious revival leaves out the most important part of it. The ignorant became readers, writers, and leaders; the indigent began working and learning to excel at their work; housewives raised their children to be good family people, citizens, and neighbors; paupers and drunks began to earn a living, to save and invest and send their children to the universities and their grandchildren to the House of Commons. An often brutal society in which a woman walking alone on the street could expect to be at least verbally molested, in which the highways were unsafe for the unarmed, in which political corruption was common, in which sexual promiscuity was the norm, had by the early years of the new century become kinder, more loving, and — dare we say it? — more Christian.

Francis Place, a radical follower of Jeremy Bentham, rose out of poverty as a poor tailor to prosperity as a clothing merchant. He intensely disliked the growing practice of Christianity in the nation, but he noticed that along with it came a dramatic change in the way people were living. Looking back from his old age, he reflected on the difference between the present climate and when he was growing up in the 1780s:

> The circumstances which it will be seen I have mentioned relative to the ignorance, the immorality, the grossness, the obscenity, the drunkenness, the dirtiness and depravity of

the middling and even of a large portion of the better sort of tradesmen, the artisans, and the journeymen tradesmen of London in the days of my youth, may excite a suspicion that the picture I have drawn is a caricature, the parts of which are out of keeping and have no symmetry as a whole.

When Alexis de Tocqueville arrived in the 1830s and observed the contrast that Place was talking about, he concluded that a great revolution had taken place in England and was still in process, but a revolution very different from those of his native France. He was particularly struck by the fact that the nobility of England were fully engaged in the reconstitution of religious and moral living that was taking over the country. Consider his account of a luncheon at the Earl of Radnor's house on May 27, 1835:

> Before coming to table Lord Radnor went to his study; Lady Radnor and his daughters went there too; after a moment eleven or twelve women and eight or ten men-servants came in. . . . These twenty people took their places round the room and knelt down looking towards the wall. Near the fireplace Lord and Lady Radnor and Lady Louisa knelt down too, and Lord Radnor read a prayer aloud, the servants giving the responses. This sort of little service lasted six or eight minutes, after which the male and female servants got up and went out in the same order to resume their work.

Of course, if that were all that had happened, just a little ceremony superimposed upon the same set of habits and relationships, it would have had little meaning. But Tocqueville observed that the culture had changed in profound ways that were symbolized by such ceremonies, and that is why he called the changes revolutionary. And Tocqueville described Lord Radnor, because of his political affiliations, as a *radical*. Everywhere Tocqueville traveled in England he saw this sort of

devotional exercise, which he knew very well he would not have seen a half-century earlier.

It was a feature of this particular religious renewal that for the most part it rejected the view that serious Christianity concerned only the individual, not the society. Although most of the major actors in the drama believed in the doctrines of Adam Smith and therefore in the efficacy and justice of free markets (the doctrine was then called "political economy"), they were anything but individualists, a charge that has often been made. They banded together in huge numbers to form societies for helping the poor, evangelizing among an amazingly diverse array of groups, reforming morals, suppressing vice, improving the lot of prisoners, rescuing prostitutes from their economic distress and therefore their bondage, distributing religious literature, and promoting foreign missions.

The number and variety of these societies will probably never be exhaustively catalogued, nor any accurate estimate be made of the multitudes that supported them with their labor and money. By 1814, the Bible society alone had more than 100,000 members and unnumbered auxiliary organizations in almost every English county. A decade later, there were more than 850 auxiliaries and 500 ladies' groups. In Manchester, Methodists formed the Strangers' Friend Society, which, in an interesting twist on the meaning of charity, served the poor of any denomination *except* Methodists. Their motto was, "As we are, so shall the stranger be before the Lord."

A veritable army was marching through England doing good, or at least trying to do good. The church visitors were the unofficial and unpaid social workers of the nation. Many clergymen had what amounted to relief agencies in the parishes, with (mainly) women taking turns visiting the sick and needy. The big national societies had local chapters making a difference in the condition of neighborhoods, towns, and hamlets. Food, clothing, and medical care, training for productive work, rescue from prostitution, and education through the ragged schools were among the wares carried in the volunteers' kits.

Children were widely abused and forced to work from a young age in Wilberforce's time.

As in the case of the national societies, evangelicals conducted most of this activity, but others took up their example as well. Even after the young men at Clapham married and began raising families in the late 1790s, they continued to give away large sums of money for these purposes. Evangelicals of all economic classes emphasized the obligation to provide generously for the needy, and when the Tractarian movement metamorphosed into Ritualism, it took root mainly in poor parishes desperate for material as well as spiritual help. One angry woman, writing to the American Unitarian leader William Ellery Channing, complained that Hannah More, by writing *Cælebs in Search of a Wife*, had made devoting two evenings a week to visiting the poor "a fashion and a rage." *Cælebs* was published in 1809, and the first ladies' auxiliary of the British and Foreign Bible Society appeared two years later, swelling the ranks of the visitors. This activity lasted decades and took innumerable forms. The Manchester Town Mission had 52 full-time workers visiting houses, urging attendance at public worship, and telling parents about the importance of securing an education for their children. Their operating funds came largely from voluntary donations from working class districts. Ellen Ranyard, an evangelical born in 1810, trained a corps of followers to help poor women manage their households, teaching them to cook, clean, and do needlework. She enrolled a group of poor women to train as itinerant nurses, and so increased the effectiveness of the other women making their rounds. She called these women "Bible nurses." Workers like Mrs. Ranyard became an example to others, and Quakers, Jews, Catholics, and others made similar efforts.

With the surge of piety and of literacy (largely through Sunday schools staffed by volunteer workers) the society was marked by an enormous appetite for Bible reading and Bible instruction. Informal study groups were active among churchmen and dissenters alike, and the printing presses were kept busy churning out Bibles and other literature for them. Autobiographical writings from the period suggest that after the Bible, the two books having the most formative effect on Englishmen were *Pilgrim's Progress* and *Paradise Lost*, themselves based on the Bible. Collections of sermons were staples among the booksellers. Some of the literature was either given away or sold at heavily subsidized prices, but there was also a thriving market-driven trade in religious books.

The interdenominational Colportage Association recruited and trained sellers of Christian literature who saw this task as a calling fully as worthy to be followed as preaching and teaching. Free and subsidized tracts and Colportage distribution still left an enormous unserved market — those who could not or would not pay for expensive books, but demanded more than tracts. The lending libraries filled the vacuum. Circulating libraries had existed from the latter half of the 18th century, but with a greatly expanded reading public they became much more important in the next century. Hannah More's

Cælebs in Search of a Wife, which went to 30 editions by the time of her death in 1834, was written explicitly for them.

C.E. Mudie (from 1842) and W.H. Smith (1858) became the largest distributors of books in the kingdom, and were in effect the arbiters of what the reading public would have available. Both were evangelicals. Mudie was a dissenter who occasionally preached and wrote hymns, and Smith considered becoming a clergyman. They judged books not only from a business perspective but also from the standpoint of their religious faith, avoiding what they considered indecency or blasphemy. Mudie affected the book purchasers' reading habits, as well as the borrowers', because of his influence over the decisions of publishers. Considering whether to publish a new novel, the publishing offices would resound with the crucial question: "What will Mudie say?"

If the religious revival turned ordinary people toward what seemed to be an older or traditional notion of moral behavior, it also affected people who wished to reform radically some of the basic institutions of the society. The Chartist leaders who sought political reform to improve the conditions of workers included among their number preachers and also legions of Bible readers, and Chartist chapels dotted the English countryside in the 1840s. Tocqueville became acquainted with many of the radical leaders and noted how different they were from their French counterparts — much more respectful of property and of religion as well, including a great number of what he called "enthusiastic sectarians," which is to say evangelical dissenters.

The radical writer Harriet Martineau was more affected by the religious revival than she ever acknowledged. Her modern biographer believes that she did not realize how indebted her thinking was to the religious doctrines that she consciously rejected. Her intense interest in the Bible as a child developed into theological pursuits, and although they did not persist, the residue of the beliefs never left her, and her criticisms of the Church of England seem little different from the standard dissenting line. An old history of socialism says that

in order to understand the radical William Godwin (1756–1836) "it must always be borne in mind that he was essentially a Calvinist preacher. His materialism is inverted Calvinist theology." That is to say, the radical content was transmitted with the moral intensity of the evangelical environment. Robert Taylor, a notorious former clergyman, delivered spell-binding radical sermons at the Blackfriars Rotunda in London, a center of militant causes. Professing himself to be an unbeliever, he preached his gospel with all the zest and emotional power of the most fervid evangelical preacher in the kingdom. He was not alone.

The pre-Victorian period we have been considering was a remarkable one because it seemed to belie the oft-repeated historicist admonition that we cannot turn back the clock. We hear this mainly from progressives who decry the resisting of trends that seem to be dominant, and who wish to continue what has been set in motion. But the impulse behind the remark is a conservative one; it wishes to preserve the trend against those who would change it. People who were setting the new agenda in the 18th century ended up creating a very different society in the 19th. Wesley and Whitefield, Venn of Huddersfield and Walker of Truro, were conscious of recreating in tiny villages or in isolated parishes the promise of a gospel that had atrophied from neglect and self-interest. As the movement spread, it coalesced around academic leaders in Cambridge and then political leaders in Clapham; it spawned publications and societies almost beyond number; it attracted the allegiance of many millions of people who accepted its claims upon them.

Then it attracted the attention of people who were critical of its shortcomings, who trained a new generation in Rugby and other public schools, in Oxford, and from there a thousand parishes. It fragmented into competing and often antagonistic schools among both Anglicans and dissenters, but the fragments were sparks, setting fires as they were scattered throughout the land. There were many differences among the fragments, but they were united on a few main principles. They were one in their rejection of the laxity and shallowness that dominated 18th-century English religion and society, the Christ-less conjunction of moralism with a deep and pervasive immorality. They all sought the recovery of the gospel that had animated the early Church, and they all believed in the seriousness of religious profession and the conduct that flowed from it.

In this remarkable renewal of vital Christianity, for all the limitations of its participants and consequent shortcomings of the movement, the tincture of vital religion spread throughout the society, giving to it the coloration of a revived Christianity. This new society, a product of a silent revolution from within its own resources, its own history and traditions, was far from perfect, but it freed the slaves, taught the ignorant, brought spiritual light where there was darkness, turned the drunk and indigent into useful citizens and effective parents, and ameliorated the harsh conditions brought about by industrialization, internal migration, and rapid population growth. It was a revolution that succeeded in making almost all things better. There are not many like that.

The lamentations about contemporary American society — indeed of Western societies in general — seem little different from those heard in the 18th century and the early years of the 19th. The empty religiosity coexisting with open contempt for the Christian heritage of the nation, the widespread hypocrisy, the general

John Wesley preaching

lawlessness, and the political corruption were similar. Change the time-specific terminology and examples in William Wilberforce's *Practical View of the Prevailing Religious System of Professed Christians* (1797) and you might think it was written two centuries later.

Yet there seemed to be remarkably little hand-wringing in Wilberforce and his merry band of anti-slavers. Full of hope, they did their duty to God and men as they were given light, braved the setbacks, and did not seem amazed at their great successes. It was as if they believed that God was ultimately in charge and they had only to be faithful to their charges. There is no reason that experience could not be repeated today, despite the widespread pessimism. After all, it was only two years from the time Bishop Butler announced to the world that Great Britain had decided that Christianity was fictitious that John Wesley found spiritual life in Christ and the renewal of the entire society began its course.

EDITOR'S NOTE:
Herbert Schlossberg is a Senior Fellow at the Ethics and Public Policy Center in Washington, D.C. This essay is based on his book, The Silent Revolution and the Making of Victorian England *(Ohio State University Press). Copyright © 2000. First Things, Issue 106 (October 2000): Pages 46-51. Reprinted by permission.*

51

1759	William Wilberforce born at Kingston-upon-Hull, Yorkshire
1760	Clarkson born at Wisbech, Cambridgeshire, March 28
1768	His father dies; sent to live in Wimbledon with an aunt and uncle
1772	Slavery abolished in England
1776	Wilberforce studies at St. John's College, Cambridge (until 1780)
1776	American colonies declare independence
1786	Clarkson's essay on slavery wins prize at Cambridge
1788	Hannah More's *Thoughts on the Manners of the Great*
1780	Robert Raikes founds the first Sunday school
1780	Elected Member of Parliament (MP) for Hull
1783	William Pitt becomes the British prime minister; war with colonies ends with British defeat at Yorktown
1784–1785	Wilberforce experiences a deep conversion
1784	Wilberforce becomes MP for Yorkshire
1787	Wilberforce helps found Society for the Reformation of Manners
1789	Wilberforce introduces his first bill to abolish the slave trade

William Wilberforce

Abolition Slave Trade

1789	French Revolution begins
1791	Wilberforce's motion to abolish slave trade loses 163-88
1792	519 petitions sent to Parliament; Dundas amendment for gradual abolition passes Commons; Lords start new inquiry
1796	*A Practical View of the Prevailing Religious System of Professed Christians . . .* is published
1797	Wilberforce marries Barbara Spooner
1804	Abolition campaign revives; a bill passes Commons
1804	Wilberforce helps found the British and Foreign Bible Society and the Church Missionary Society
1806	185 ships carry 43,755 slaves to America
1806	William Pitt dies; Grenville forms new administration; ban on slave trade to captured colonies passes both houses
1807	British Parliament abolishes slave trade
1807	The United States abolishes importation of slaves
1811	London becomes first city with more than one million citizens; disease, overcrowding, and crime are rife
1813	Wilberforce helps convince Parliament to permit missionaries to India

1815	Wellington defeats Napoleon at Waterloo; France agrees to abolish slave trade; Portugal follows suit
1820	Spain becomes last major European power to abolish its slave trade
1821	Elizabeth Fry establishes the British Society for Promoting the Reformation of Female Prisoners
1822	Wilberforce helps form the Anti-Slavery Society
1823	Wilberforce launches campaign for emancipation of slaves
1825	Wilberforce retires from the House of Commons
1831	Lord's Day Observance Society founded
1833	Emancipation Act is passed: all slaves in the British Dominions granted freedom; Wilberforce dies and is buried at Westminster Abbey
1833	Lord Althrop's Factory Act mitigates child labor
1837	Victoria becomes queen of Great Britain (reigns until 1901)
1842	The Mines Act abolishes all female labor in the mines
1844-1847	Factory acts reduce daily work hours to six for children and ten for adults
1846	Clarkson dies

William Wilberforce

1845-1846 Potato blight leads to famine in Ireland; one million people die and thousands immigrate to America

1848-1849 Revolutions sweep Europe; cholera epidemic kills 14,000 people (10,000 in London) and precipitates municipal sanitation.

1853-1856 Britain, France, and Piedmont defeat Russia in the Crimean War

1860 Florence Nightingale's *Notes on Nursing*

1864 Shaftesbury introduces measures to forbid the employment of boys under ten as chimney sweeps

1867 Thomas Barnardo (1845–1905) opens his first children's home in London slums

1869 Debtors' prisons abolished

1870 Foster's Education Act promotes a national system of elementary education

1871 Removal of religious tests at Oxford and Cambridge allows Nonconformists to attend

1872 Licensing Act controls the sale of alcohol

1875 Artisans Dwellings Act aims to provide better houses for the poor

1878 William Booth (1829–1912) founds the Salvation Army

[1] Courtesy of *Christian History* – Issue 53 (Vol.XVI, No1), revised by Andrew Parker

In the 1400s, Europe began discovering the great mass of Africa beyond the vast Sahara. At the end of the century, it also discovered the Americas. Little did it know that the two land masses would become so inextricably bound.

For the next two centuries, European superpowers planted a chain of European colonies from New England to the West Indies to Brazil. Such places seemed to have an inexhaustable supply of sugar, tobacco, silver, and gold. Visions of great wealth danced before the superpowers' eyes — provided they could find the labor to exploit the situation.

They soon concluded that such labor could not be found in the Americas. The "redskins" in the North refused to abandon a nomadic lifestyle based on hunting to pick cotton on white men's plantations. The natives of Central and South America didn't seem physically capable of the work their conquerors expected of them. Yet somehow, civilized Europe was determined to have its sweets, tobacco, and other exotic commodities.

Twenty Black Slaves

The solution came from Portuguese traders who had found something in Africa besides gold. In 1440, the first cargo brought to Lisbon by the first European company for the exploitation of West Africa consisted of 20 black slaves. The Portuguese concluded that if blacks could work in Portugal, they could work in Brazil. To the Portuguese, these Africans were simple, childlike folk, docile, inured to tropical heat, strong, tough — they seemed to have been created for the special needs of colonial planters.

Nor was it particularly difficult or dangerous to get them. In fact, they could be gotten more easily than gold or ivory.

So, in due course, men, women, and children from West Africa were bundled across the ocean not just by the Portuguese but by all of Europe's superpowers, and not in tens or hundreds, but in thousands and tens of thousands. Life and commerce in the Americas had been saved, so to speak, by a transfusion of blood from Africa.

From 1660 onward, English statesmen steadily encouraged the expansion of the slave trade as a key factor in the country's commercial and naval strength. Forts were built on the African "Gold Coast," from Cape Verde to the Gulf of Guinea, and in 1713 a treaty with Spain transferred from French to English merchants the notorious Asiento, the monopoly of the supply of slaves to the Spanish colonies.

The trade grew quickly. By the early 1700s, English traders dumped about 25,000 Africans on the other side of the Atlantic every year. By about 1770, it had risen to 50,000, half of what all Europe exported. By 1787, the numbers were down, but Britain was still the European leader in transports, with 38,000 slaves annually (France was second with 31,000).

Season of Terror

The season of the coming of the slave ships was a season of terror and violence all along the Gold Coast, or "hunting-ground," as the traders called it. The slaves were obtained in three ways: by seizure, by purchase from professional traders, or by barter with a chief.

A PROFITABLE LITTLE BUSINESS BY MARK GALLI

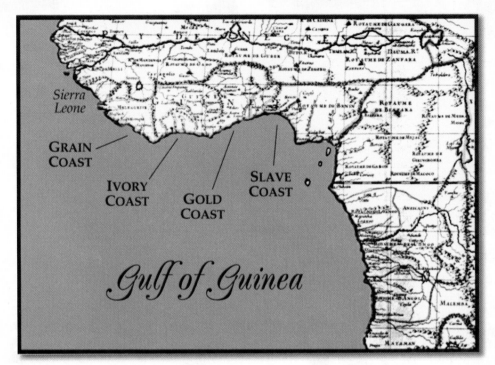

Pictured are the principal areas from which slavers captured Africans.

Professional traders were mostly Arabs of old-established firms, which had carried on the traffic in the heart of Africa for ages past. They captured their slaves in the interior and brought them to the coast for sale.

A deal with a native chief was the easiest and most productive method. British agents were sent to the interior with orders "to encourage the chieftains by brandy and gunpowder to go to war and make slaves." A chief was rarely found who could hold out against such "encouragement." The usual result: the chief ordered his soldiers to round up a neighboring village at night and bring back all the captives. Sometimes, if his greed were desperate, a chief sold his own subjects into slavery.

If there were raids, then there were reprisals. Chief went to war with chief and tribe with tribe. Victory meant wealth, and defeat meant slavery.

With their holds filled by one means or another with living cargo, slave ships set sail for the West. Peace, at least for a season, settled down again on West Africa. But villages lay wrecked and empty among the neglected corn, and childless parents and orphaned children grieved.

The Miserable Passage

The sufferings of Africans had only just begun. The voyage to the West Indies could take three or four weeks, or more in unfavorable weather. The route to the West Indies was entirely within the tropical belt. For the slaves in the small sailing ships, this "Middle Passage" was an inferno.

Caught in the Act

The bigger the cargo, the bigger the profit. A boat of 100 to 150 tons could carry 300 to 600 slaves. Five feet of space separated the decks. Male slaves were laid on the floor and on shelves, manacled

If the slave ship visited an unfrequented part of the coast, or if inhabitants could be taken by surprise, a sudden armed landing was made and Africans were kidnapped.

The meanest treachery was regarded by some slave captains as legitimate business practice. On one occasion, the British military governor of Goree was entertaining a party of over a hundred natives — men, women, and children — who were thoroughly enjoying themselves in dance and song. Three slave captains with him suggested that the whole party be seized and carried off to their ships. They claimed that a former governor, on a similar occasion, had consented to just such an act.

together in pairs, sometimes so closely packed they had to lay on their sides in sultry heat and rank air. Abruptly torn from their homes, wholly unused to the sea, they lay terrified by the mystery of what was to become of them.

Diagram of the slave ship Brookes

They were fed the coarsest food. Numbers fell ill. Dysentery was rife. In fine weather, they would be taken on deck for a time and forced to dance in their chains, for exercise, while their quarters below were cleaned. In rough weather, they had to remain below. Conditions in a severe Atlantic gale of some days' duration would multiply their sufferings. It is a wonder that only up to a quarter of the slaves died on the voyage. But it is not a wonder that sometimes an African, temporarily released from his fetters, would leap into the sea.

Women and children were not chained together or packed so closely. But the women were regularly exposed to sailors' lust and children to sailors' cruelty. John Newton often told about a mate "who threw a child overboard because it moaned at night in its mother's arms and kept him awake."

Ironically, the slaves were not the only sufferers. Brutal treatment of crews was more or less a regular part of the sailor's life at sea. Add to that the inescapable disease on such ships, and we can understand why the death rate among the white men engaged in the slave trade was far higher than in any other merchant service. We can also understand why, at times, captains of slave ships seized young British men from the street or from gambling parlors and force them to crew on slave ships.

Toward the end of the voyage, slaves were examined and prepared for sale. Wounds were doctored and, as far as possible, concealed. But all traces of the Middle Passage could not always be removed. Agents' reports at the ports in the early records are full of complaints: "The parcel of Negroes were very mean." "Very bad, being much abused." "These . . . included some little boys and dying Negroes." Strong men were singly and quickly disposed of at good prices — as much as £40 apiece — but the sick and injured would be lumped with women and children in a batch and sold off at a discount — such were called "refuse."

Then began the next chapter in a life of servitude.

Vested Interests

All Englishmen in the 1700s, whatever their faults, were not devilishly cruel. How could they tolerate this state of affairs? First, the harsh facts of slavery were not widely known. Second, the public knew as little and cared as little about Africans as "Indians." It demanded an unusual effort of imagination to comprehend the sufferings of remote foreigners.

But why did the leaders of church and state, many of whom knew very well what was going on, do nothing?

First, the slave trade was a profitable business. Liverpool slavers, for instance, between 1783 and 1793, carried over 300,000 slaves to the West Indies, sold them for over £15,000,000, and pocketed a net profit of 30 percent. The productivity of the West Indies was on the line. "The impossibility of doing without slaves in the West Indies," wrote a London publicist in 1764, "will always prevent this traffic being dropped. The necessity, the absolute necessity, then, of carrying it on, must, since there is no other, be its excuse."

TO BE SOLD on board the Ship *Bance-Island*, on tuesday the 6th of *May* next, at *Ashley-Ferry*, a choice cargo of about 250 fine healthy

NEGROES,

just arrived from the Windward & Rice Coast. —The utmost care has already been taken, and shall be continued, to keep them free from the least danger of being infected with the SMALL-POX, no boat having been on board, and all other communication with people from *Charles-Town* prevented.

Austin, Laurens, & Appleby.

N. B. Full one Half of the above Negroes have had the SMALL-POX in their own Country.

Poster for new slave arrivals

Second, there were reasons of state. If Britain withdrew from so large a field in the slave trade, it would put her maritime strength, at least compared with her European rivals, in jeopardy. Besides, any interference with the trade by England would arouse the bitterest resentment in the colonies. It was also argued that filling up the islands with slaves would keep them more loyal to the mother country — lest they become like those tiresome New England colonies, which developed into little democracies of white men with English notions of political freedom.

And so the slave agents, colonial planters, naval officers, and officials of state became a powerful vested interest. These "West Indians" became a formidable body in politics and society, and it would be a bold man who would face their influence and wrath. But the silence of consent did not remain unbroken. No sooner had the trade firmly established itself and the vested interests felt secure than individual protesters began to make themselves heard.

EDITOR'S NOTE:

Mark Galli is editor of Christian History. This article is an adaptation of a chapter from Reginald Coupland's Wilberforce (Collins, 1945). It is used by permission.

EDITOR'S NOTE:
This extract, taken from chapter 2 of the Interesting Narrative, *describes the young Equiano's forced entry into a slave ship on the coast of Africa. "Middle Passage": the journey between Africa and the New World. Equiano's passage is between West Africa and the Caribbean island of Barbados, at that time a common voyage as the British plantation island was among the most easterly of the Caribbean islands.*

The first object which saluted my eyes when I arrived on the coast was the sea, and a slave-ship, which was then riding at anchor, and waiting for its cargo. These filled me with astonishment, which was soon converted into terror, which I am yet at a loss to describe, nor the then feelings of my mind. When I was carried on board, I was immediately handled, and tossed up, to see if I were sound, by some of the crew; and, I was now persuaded that I was got into a world of bad spirits, and that they were going to kill me. Their complexions too differing, so much from ours, their long hair, and the language they spoke, which was very different from any I had ever heard, united to confirm me in this belief. Indeed, such were the horrors of my views and fears at the moment, that, if ten thousand worlds had been my own, I would have freely parted with them all, to have exchanged my condition with that of the meanest slave in my own country. When I looked round the ship too, and saw a large furnace of copper boiling, and a multitude of black people of every description chained together, every

Olaudah Equiano

one of their countenances expressing dejection and sorrow, I no longer doubted of my fate, and, quite overpowered with horror and anguish, I fell motionless on the deck and fainted. When I recovered a little, I found some black people about me, who I believed were some of those who brought me on board, and had been receiving their pay. They talked to me in order to cheer me, but all in vain. I asked them if we were not to be eaten by those white men with horrible looks, red faces, and long hair? They told me I was not; and one of the crew brought me a small portion of spirituous liquor in a wine glass; but, being afraid of him, I would not take it out his hand. One of the blacks therefore took it from him and gave it to me, and I took a little down my palate, which, instead of reviving me, as they thought it would, threw me into the greatest consternation at the strange feeling it produced, having never tasted any such liquor before. Soon after this, the blacks, who brought me on board, went off and left me abandoned to despair. I now saw myself deprived of all chance of returning to my native country, or even the least glimpse of hope of gaining the shore, which I now considered as friendly: and, I even wished for my former slavery in preference to my present situation, which was filled with horrors of every kind, still heightened by my ignorance of what I was to undergo. I was not long suffered to indulge my grief; I was soon put down under the decks, and there I received such a salutation in my nostrils as I had never experienced

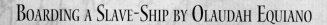

BOARDING A SLAVE-SHIP BY OLAUDAH EQUIANO

A slave ship boarding slaves

I naturally feared that element the first time I saw it; yet, nevertheless, could I have got over the nettings, I would have jumped over the side, but I could not; and, besides, the crew used to watch us very closely who were not chained down to the decks, lest we should leap into the water; and, I have seen some of these poor African prisoners most severely cut for attempting to do so, and hourly whipped for not eating. This indeed was often the case with myself. In a little time after, amongst the poor chained men, I found some of my own nation, which in a small degree gave ease to my mind. I inquired of these what was to be done with us? They gave me to understand we were to be carried to these white people's country to work for them. I was then a little revived, and thought, if it were no worse than working, my situation was not so desperate: but, still I feared I should be put to death, the white people looked and acted, as I thought, in so savage a manner; for I had never seen among any people such instances of brutal cruelty; and, this not only shewn towards us blacks, but also

in my life; so that with the loathsomeness of the stench, and crying together, I became so sick and low that I was not able to eat, nor had I the least desire to taste any thing. I now wished for the last friend, Death, to relieve me; but soon, to my grief, two of the white men offered me eatables; and, on refusing to eat, one of them held me fast by the hands, and laid me across, I think, the windlass, and tied my feet, while the other flogged me severely. I had never experienced any thing of this kind before; and, although, not being used to the water, to some of the whites themselves. One white man in particular I saw, when we were permitted to be on deck, flogged so unmercifully with a large rope near the foremast that he died in consequence of it; and, they tossed him over the side, as they would have done a brute. This made me fear these people the more; and, I expected nothing less than to be treated in the same manner.

National Maritime Museum, London

Inside a slave ship

died, thus falling victims to the improvident avarice, as I may call it, of their purchasers. This wretched situation was again aggravated by the galling of the chains, now become insupportable; and, the filth of the necessary tubs, into which the children often fell, and were almost suffocated. The shrieks of the women, and the groans of the dying, rendered the whole a scene of horror almost inconceivable. Happily perhaps for myself I was soon reduced so low here that

The Middle Passage

At last, when the ship we were in had got in all her cargo, they made ready with many fearful noises, and we were all put under deck, so that we could not see how they managed the vessel. But, this disappointment was the least of my sorrow. The stench of the hold while we were on the coast was so intolerably loathsome, that it was dangerous to remain there for any time, and some of us had been permitted to stay on the deck for the fresh air; but now that the whole ship's cargo were confined together, it became absolutely pestilential. The closeness of the place, and the heat of the climate, added to the number in the ship, which was so crowded that each had scarcely room to turn himself almost suffocated us. This produced copious perspirations, so that the air soon became unfit for respiration, from a variety of loathsome smells, and brought on a sickness among the slaves, of which many

it was thought necessary to keep me almost always on deck; and from my extreme youth I was not put in fetters. In this situation, I expected every hour to share the fate of my companions, some of whom were almost daily brought upon deck at the point of death, which I began to hope would soon put an end to my miseries. Often did I think many of the inhabitants of the deep much more happy than myself; I envied them the freedom they enjoyed, and as often wished I could change my condition for theirs. Every circumstance I met with served only to render my state more painful, and heighten my apprehensions, and my opinion of the cruelty of the whites. One day they had taken a number of fishes; and, when they had killed and satisfied themselves with as many as they thought fit, to our astonishment who were on the deck, rather than give any of them to us to eat, as we expected, they tossed the remaining fish into the sea again, although we begged and prayed for some as well we could, but in vain; and some of my countrymen, being pressed by hunger, took an opportunity, when they thought no one saw them, of trying to get a little privately; but they were discovered, and the attempt procured them some very severe floggings.

One day, when we had a smooth sea, and a moderate wind, two of my wearied countrymen, who were chained together (I was near them at the time), preferring death to such a life of misery, somehow made through the nettings, and jumped into the sea: immediately another quite dejected fellow, who, on account of his illness, was suffered to be out of irons, also followed their example; and I believe many more would soon have done the same, if they had not been prevented by the ship's crew, who were instantly alarmed. Those of us that were the most active were, in a moment, put down under the deck; and there was such a noise and confusion amongst the people of the ship as I never heard before, to stop here, and get the boat to go out after the slaves. However, two of the wretches were drowned, but they got the other, and afterwards flogged him unmercifully, for thus attempting to prefer death to slavery. In this manner, we continued to undergo more hardships than I can now relate; hardships which are inseparable from this accursed trade. Many a time we were near suffocation, from the want of fresh air, which we were often without for whole days together. This, and the stench of the necessary tubs, carried off many.

During our passage I first saw flying fishes, which surprised me very much: they used frequently to fly across the ship, and many of them fell on the deck. I also now first saw the use of the quadrant. I had often with astonishment seen the mariners make observations with it, and I could not think what it meant. They at last took notice of my surprise; and one of them, willing to increase it, as well as to gratify my curiosity, made me one day look through it. The clouds appeared to me to be land, which disappeared as they passed along. This heightened my wonder: and I was now more persuaded than ever that I was in another world, and that every thing about me was magic. At last, we came in sight of the island of Barbados, at which the whites on board gave a great shout, and made many signs of joy to us.

Africans rescued from the British slave ship Undine.

EDITOR'S NOTE:

This excerpt, taken from chapter 5 of the Interesting Narrative *by former slave Olaudah Equiano, describes the abuse of slaves in the West Indies. It was this account and others that was said to have greatly influenced William Wilberforce's passion for abolishing the slave trade.*

While I was thus, employed by my master, I was often a witness to cruelties of every kind, which were exercised on my unhappy fellow slaves. I used frequently to have different cargoes of new Negroes in my care for sale; and it was almost a constant practice with our clerks, and other whites, to commit violent depredations on the chastity of the female slaves; and these I was, though with reluctance, obliged to submit to at all times, being unable to help them. When we have had some of these slaves on board my master's vessel, to carry them to other islands, or to America, I have known oar mates to commit these acts most shamefully, to the disgrace, not of Christians only, but of men. I have even known them to

Slave shed where African captives were held until sold into slavery

gratify their brutal passion with females not ten years old; and, these abominations, some of them practiced to such scandalous excess, that one of our captains discharged the mate and others on that account. And yet, in Montserrat I have seen a Negro man staked to the ground, and cut most shockingly, and then his ears cut off bit by bit, because he had been connected with a white woman, who was a common prostitute. As if it were no crime in the whites to rob an innocent African girl of her virtue; but most heinous in a black man only to gratify a passion of nature, where the temptation was offered by one of a different color, though the most abandoned woman of her species. One Mr. D — told me that he had sold 41,000 Negroes, and that he once cut off a Negro man's leg for running away. I asked him if the man had died in the operation, how he, as a Christian, could answer for the horrid act before God? And he told me, answering was a thing of another world, what he thought and did were policy. I told him that the Christian doctrine taught us to do unto others as we would that others should do unto us. He then said that his scheme had the desired effect: it cured that man and some others of running away.

Another Negro man was half hanged, and then burnt, for attempting to poison a cruel overseer. Thus, by repeated cruelties, are the wretched first urged to despair, and then murdered, because they still retain so much of human nature about them as to wish to put an end to their misery, and retaliate on their tyrants. These overseers are indeed for the most part persons of the worst character of any denomination of men in the West Indies. Unfortunately, many humane gentlemen, but not residing on their estates, are obliged to leave the management of them in the hands of these human butchers, who cut and mangle the slaves in a shocking manner on the most trifling occasions, and altogether treat them in every respect like brutes. They pay no regard to the situation of pregnant women, nor the least attention to the lodging of the field Negroes. Their huts, which ought to be well covered, and the place dry where they take their little repose, are often open sheds, built in damp places; so that when the poor creatures return tired from the toils of the field, they contract many disorders, from being exposed to the damp air in this uncomfortable state, while they are heated, and their pores are open.

This neglect certainly conspires with many others to cause a decrease in the births as well as in the lives of the grown Negroes. I can quote many instances of gentlemen, who reside on their estates in the West Indies, and then the scene is quite changed; the Negroes are treated with lenity and proper care, by which their lives are prolonged, and their masters profited. To the honor of humanity, I knew several gentlemen who managed their estates in this manner, and they found that benevolence was their true interest. And, among many I could mention in several of the islands, I knew one in Montserrat whose slaves looked remarkably well, and never needed any fresh supplies of Negroes; and, there are many other estates, especially in Barbados, which, from such judicious treatment, need no fresh stock of Negroes at any time. I have the honor of knowing a most worthy and humane gentleman, who is a native of Barbados, and has estates there. This gentleman has written a treatise on the usage of his own slaves. He allows them two hours of refreshment at mid-day, and many other indulgencies and comforts, particularly in their lodging; and, besides this, he raises more provisions on his estate than they can destroy; so that by these attentions, he saves the lives of his Negroes, and keeps them healthy, and as happy as the condition of slavery can admit. I

Slaves being marched to the ships

North Wind Picture Archives

myself, as shall appear in the sequel, managed an estate, where, by those attentions, the Negroes were uncommonly cheerful and healthy, and did more work by half than by the common mode of treatment they usually do. For want, therefore, of such care and attention to the poor Negroes, and otherwise oppressed as they are, it is no wonder that the decrease should require 20,000 new Negroes annually, to fill up the vacant places of the dead.

Even in Barbados, notwithstanding those humane exceptions which I have mentioned, and others I am acquainted with, which justly make it quoted as a place where slaves meet with the best treatment and need fewest recruits of any in the West Indies, yet this island requires 1,000 Negroes annually to keep up the original stock, which is only 90,000. So that the whole term of a Negro's life may be said to be there but sixteen years! Also yet the climate here in every respect is the same as that from which they are taken, except in being more wholesome. Do the British colonies decrease in this manner? And yet, what prodigious difference is there between an English and West India climate?

While I was in Montserrat I knew a Negro man, named Emanuel Sankey, who endeavored to escape from his miserable bondage, by concealing himself on board of a London ship, but fate did not favor the poor oppressed man; for, being discovered when the vessel was under sail, he was delivered up again to his master. This Christian master immediately pinned the wretch down to the ground at each wrist and ankle, and then took some sticks of sealing wax, and lighted them, and dropped it all over his back. There was another master who was noted for cruelty; and, I believe he had not a slave but what had been cut, and had pieces fairly taken out of the flesh. And after they had been punished thus, he used

to make them get into a long wooden box or case he had for that purpose, in which he shut them up during pleasure. It was just about the height and breadth of a man; and the poor wretches had no room, when in the case, to move.

It was very common in several of the islands, particularly in St. Kitt's, for the slaves to be branded with the initial letters of their master's name; and, a load of heavy iron hooks hung about their necks. Indeed, on the most trifling occasions, they were loaded with chains; and often instruments of torture were added. The iron muzzle, thumb-screws, etc., are so well known, as not to need a description, and were sometimes applied for the slightest faults. I have seen a Negro beaten till some of his bones were broken, for only letting a pot boil over. Is it surprising that usage like this should drive the poor creatures to despair, and make them seek a refuge in death from those evils which render their lives intolerable? While,

With shudd'ring horror pale, and eyes aghast,
They view their lamentable lot, and find
No rest?

This they frequently do. A Negro man, on board a vessel of my master, while I belonged to her, having been put in irons for some trifling misdemeanor, and kept in that state for some days, being weary of life, took an opportunity of jumping overboard into the sea; however, he was picked up without being drowned. Another, whose life was also a burden to him, resolved to starve himself to death, and refused to eat any victuals. This procured him a severe flogging; and he also, on the first occasion, which offered, jumped overboard at Charleston, but was saved.

"So much misery, condensed in so little room, is more than the human imagination had ever before conceived."
– William Wilberforce

The Amazing Grace of Freedom

Nor is there any greater regard shown to the little property, than there is to the persons and lives of the Negroes. I have already related an instance or two of particular oppression out of many which I have witnessed; but the following is frequent in all the islands. The wretched field-slaves, after toiling all the day for an unfeeling owner, who gives then but little victuals, steal sometimes a few moments from rest or refreshment to gather some small portion of grass, according as their time will admit. This they commonly tie up in a parcel; either a bit's worth (sixpence) or half a bit's worth, and bring it to town, or to the market, to sell. Nothing is more common than for the white people on this occasion to take the grass from them without paying for it; and, not only so, but too often also, to my knowledge, our clerks, and many others, at the same time have committed acts of violence on the poor, wretched, and helpless females; whom I have seen for hours stand crying to no purpose, and get no redress or pay of any kind. Is not this one common and crying sin enough to bring down God's judgment on the islands? He tells us the oppressor and the oppressed are both in his hands; and, if these are not the poor, the broken-hearted, the blind, the captive, to be bruised, which our Saviour speaks of, who are they? . . .

The small account in which the life of a Negro is held in the West Indies, is so universally known, that it might seem impertinent to quote the following extract, if some people had not been hardy enough of late to assert that Negroes are on the same footing in that respect as Europeans. By the 329th Act, page 125, of the Assembly of Barbados, it is enacted "That if any Negro, or other slave, under punishment by his master, or his order, for running away, or any other crime or misdemeanor towards his said master, unfortunately shall suffer in life or member, no person whatsoever shall be

Here a slave is pictured in the slave traders' version of handcuffs.

liable to a fine; but if any person shall, out of wantonness, or only of bloody-mindedness, or cruel intention, willfully kill a Negro, or other slave, of his own, he shall pay into the public treasury fifteen pounds sterling." And, it is the same in most, if not all of the West India islands. Is not this one of the many acts of the islands, which call loudly for redress? And do not the assembly which enacted it deserve the appellation of savages and brutes, rather than of Christians and men? It is an act at once unmerciful, unjust, and unwise; which for cruelty would disgrace an assembly of those who are called barbarians; and, for its injustice and insanity would shock the morality and common sense of a Samaide or Hottentot.

Shocking as this and many other acts of the bloody West India code at first view appear, how is the iniquity of it heightened when we consider to whom it may be extended! Mr. James Tobin, a zealous laborer in the vineyard of slavery, gives an account of a French planter of his acquaintance in the island of Martinico, who showed him many mulattoes working in the field like beasts of burden; and, he told Mr. Tobin these were all the produce of his own loins! And, I myself have known similar instances. Pray, reader, are these sons and daughters of the French planter less his children by being the progeny of black women? And, what must be the virtue of those legislators, and the feelings of those fathers, who estimate the lives of their sons, however begotten, at no more than fifteen pounds; though they should be murdered, as the act says, out of wantonness and bloody-mindedness! But, is not the slave trade entirely at war with the heart of man? And, surely that which is begun by breaking down the barriers of virtue, involves in its continuance destruction to every principle, and buries all sentiment in ruin!

I have often seen slaves, particularly those who were meagre, in different islands, put into scales and weighed, and then sold from three pence to six pence or nine pence a pound. My master, however, whose humanity was shocked at this mode, used to sell such by the lumps. And at or after a sale, it was not uncommon to see Negroes taken from their wives, wives taken from their husbands, and children from their parents,

A slave rebellion in the late 1700s in Santo Domingo sent a wave of fear through Parliament and stalled abolitionists' efforts.

and sent off to other islands, and wherever else their merciless lords choose; and probably never more during life see each other! Oftentimes my heart has bled at these partings, when the friends of the departed have been at the water side, and with sighs and tears, have kept their eyes fixed on the vessel, till it went out of sight.

A poor Creole Negro, I knew well, who, after having been often thus transported from island to island, at last resided in Montserrat. This man used to tell me many melancholy tales of himself. Generally, after he had done working for his master, he used to employ his few leisure moments to go fishing. When he had caught any fish, his master would frequently take them from him without paying him; and, at other times some other white people would serve him in the same manner. One day he said to me, very movingly, "Sometimes when a white man take away my fish, I go to my maser, and he get me my right; and when my maser by strength take away my fishes,

Collection Viollet

what me must do? I can't go to any body to be righted; then," said the poor man, looking up above, "I must look up to God Almighty, in the top, for right." This artless tale moved me much, and I could not help feeling the just cause Moses had in redressing his brother against the Egyptian. I exhorted the man to look up still to the God on the top, since there was no redress below. Though I little thought then that I myself should more than once experience such imposition, and need the same exhortation hereafter, in my own transactions in the islands, and that even this poor man and I should some time after suffer together in the same manner, as shall be related hereafter.

Nor was such usage as this confined to particular places or individuals; for, in all the different islands in which I have been, (and I have visited no less than fifteen), the treatment of the slaves was nearly the same; so nearly, indeed, that the history of an island, or even a plantation, with a few such exceptions as I have mentioned, might serve for a history of the whole. Such a tendency has the slave trade to debauch men's minds, and harden them to every feeling of humanity! For I will not suppose that the dealers in slaves are born worse than other men. No, such is the fatality of this mistaken avarice, that it corrupts the milk of human kindness and turns it into gall. And, had the pursuits of those men been different, they might have been as generous, as tender-hearted and just, as they are unfeeling, rapacious, and cruel. Surely this traffic cannot be good, which spreads like a pestilence, and taints what it touches! Which violates that first natural right of mankind, equality and independency, and gives one man a dominion over his fellows which God could never intend! For it raises the owner to a state as far above man as it depresses the slave below it; and, with all the presumption of human pride, sets a distinction between them, immeasurable in extent, and endless in duration! Yet how mistaken is the avarice even of the planters. Are slaves more useful by being thus humbled to the condition of brutes, than they would be if suffered to enjoy the privileges of men? The freedom, which diffuses health and prosperity throughout Britain,

answers you, No. When you make men slaves, you deprive them of half their virtue, you set them, in your own conduct, an example of fraud, rapine, and cruelty, and compel them to live with you in a state of war; and yet you complain that they are not honest or faithful! You stupefy them with stripes, and think it necessary to keep them in a state of ignorance. And yet, you assert that they are incapable of learning; that their minds are such a barren soil or moor, that culture would be lost on them; and that they come from a climate, where nature, though prodigal of her bounties in a degree unknown to yourselves, has left man alone scant and unfinished, and incapable of enjoying the treasures she has poured out for him! An assertion at once, impious and absurd. Why do you use those instruments of torture? Are they fit to be applied by one rational being to another? And, are ye not struck with shame and mortification, to see the partakers of your nature reduced so low? But, above all, are there no dangers attending this mode of treatment? Are you not hourly in dread of an insurrection? Nor would it be surprising; for when

No peace is given to us enslav'd, but custody severe,
And stripes and arbitrary punishment
Inflicted? What peace can we return?
But to our power, hostility and hate;
Untam'd reluctance, and revenge, though slow.
Yet ever plotting how the conqueror least
May reap his conquest, and may least rejoice
In doing what we most ill suffering feel.

But, by changing your conduct, and treating your slaves as men, every cause of fear would be banished. They would be faithful, honest, intelligent, and vigorous; and peace, prosperity, and happiness would attend you.

FAITH IN ACTION

Insights into the Biography and Character of William
Wilberforce and into His Contemporaries: Men and Women of
Faith and Values Who Reformed England and the World

*"A trade founded in iniquity, and carried on as this was, must be abolished, let the
policy be what it might — let the consequences be what they would."*
– William Wilberforce

stopping a practice which violates all the real rights of human nature.

W

illiam Wilberforce, not a name that is a household name in America, was British-born and lived his life in England.

Wilberforce was a remarkable man. He was a man who had a few outstanding gifts. One of those was that he was an accomplished speaker. He worked at improving it diligently, indefatigably, for many years. In fact, his work ethic would put most anybody I know to shame. For example, he made a chart of each hour of every day, and broke it down in quarter-hour segments. He indicated in these quarter-hour segments on the chart the time he spent in the Word of God; the time he spent in prayer; the time he spent reading; and the time he spent working toward the great goal he had felt called in his life to achieve, which was to end the slave trade.

When he was converted, one of the first things he did was go to his tailor. He told the tailor he wanted to double the number of pockets in his coats. I think he had eight pockets put in each of his coats. He wanted more pockets in his coats so he could carry more books with him, because he felt it was important to redeem every minute in study and in work for the kingdom of God.

Wilberforce worked at learning how to speak. Already gifted in that direction, he worked on his declamation every day. It was not unusual for many of the greats of the 18th and 19th centuries, both in America and Great Britain and other places, to stand before a mirror where they would speak for hours, leaning how to improve their speaking. That is called declamation. This is how he learned to speak more eloquently.

In appearance, he was four foot, eleven inches; he was slightly hunchbacked; his head was always down on his chest and turned slightly to one side. That was William Wilberforce, who changed the world. One day, when he was running for Parliament, the people couldn't see him, so somebody set him up on a table. A reporter watching it said, "They put a shrimp up on the table. But as I watched and listened to him, he turned into a whale, a giant of a man."

Wilberforce had a face that was cherubic, beautiful eyes, a most winsome voice, and a huge, caring heart. However, he wasn't always that way. He was blessed. His grandfather left him a fortune; his uncle left him another one. He was one of the wealthiest people in England. He hobnobbed in his younger years with all of the greats. He was an intimate friend of the prime minister and with earls and knights, and was very much desired in all kinds of social activities. He was not a Christian, though he was an Anglican at the time. Religion meant nothing to him, really, and as was the case, there was great nominalism in the Church of England at that time.

Born in 1759, Wilberforce was very worldly, charming, witty, a friendly kind of young man. When he was about 25, his mother said that she would like to spend the summer on a tour of Europe. Wilberforce decided to go along and invited one of his old school teachers by the name of Isaac Milner to go with him. Milner, a Christian, suggested to Wilberforce that they read Philip Doddridge's wonderful devotional classic called *The Rise and Progress of Religion* as their carriage wended its way through the countries of Europe. This had a big impact on Wilberforce, and he thought about becoming a Christian, but he said if he did, he feared he would lose all of his invitations to the best parties in England — so he decided against it.

The following summer he decided to take another trip by himself without his mother, who watched over him very carefully, because she was concerned for his well being. She did not want him to become too religious — for similar reasons, no doubt, because of his standing in the elite community of Great Britain.

Converted to Christ

He did invite Isaac Milner to go again with him. This time Milner decided that they would read the Bible on their trip across the continent. Of course, they would read the Greek New Testament, as every reasonably well-educated Englishmen at the time could do. So, they were going along reading the Bible — and the very Word of God pierced this young man's heart, and he was converted to Christ.

Isaac Milner

When Wilberforce returned home, his transformed life caused great shock. His friends said that he had lost his mind, he had become mad, and he was melancholy. That was the rumor, but when they saw him, he was the least melancholy man they had ever seen in their lives. Instead, he was filled with joy and also was even more considerate and compassionate and loving. In fact, he was seen to be the most

compassionate and loving man in all of England. The people were curious of what had happened to him.

Elected to Parliament at age 21, Wilberforce decided that now that he was a Christian, he should resign his position and do something less secular, more religious, but not until he shared his feelings with his friend William Pitt. At the time, Pitt and Wilberforce had begun their crusade in Parliament to abolish the slave trade, so he asked Wilberforce if he wanted to preach or if he wanted to change the world.

Conflicted now with the challenge Pitt had offered him, Wilberforce decided to go see John Newton, a former captain of a slave ship that brought slaves from the west coast of Africa to America and to England. When Wilberforce lived with his evangelical relatives, his uncle and aunt, the senior William Wilberforce and his wife Hannah, he had heard Newton tell the stories of how he was converted during a great storm at sea, and had accepted Christ. He became a wonderful minister and the writer of the great hymn "Amazing Grace," probably the most popular Christian hymn in the entire world. "Amazing Grace! How sweet the sound, that saved a wretch like me!"

Lifetime Crusade

Newton told him, "Do not leave your position in Parliament. You would be deserting the calling that God has called you to." So he decided not to resign his position.

Wilberforce decided he would give his life to the cause of ending slavery in Great Britain. Aware that Great Britian was not ready to abolish slavery, he knew the first step was to abolish the slave trade . . . after that the emancipation of the slaves throughout the British Colonies. Keep in mind that the British Colonies were a kingdom that the sun never set upon. It extended all over the world, from England all the way across to Canada and America, over into the Orient, and the lands over there — Hong Kong and others — down into the South seas, over to South America, to Central America, and all of Africa. The British Empire was huge, and there were many millions of slaves, but there was hardly a part of English business that wasn't wrapped around slavery in some way or another. Wilberforce was determined to end it.

He decided he would give a talk, and he spent two years studying and preparing to give that talk. When he finally stood up in Parliament to speak, he spoke for four and a half hours, and introduced a bill to end the slave trade in Great Britain. Although the bill was soundly defeated, he did not give up.

He came back the next year, gave another speech, made the motion again, and again it was defeated; next year, defeated; the next year, defeated. He skipped a year, then came back the following year, and gave another speech, and another and another and another — for two decades! Finally, the bill was passed and the British slave trade ended.

But that was only half of his goal. His goal was to end slavery in *all* of the British colonies, so he set

Northwest view of Westminster Abbey

himself to that. He continued his battle, which was to last another 25 years. Now an elderly man, he continued to pray and work, for there were still hundreds of thousands of slaves throughout the British Empire and beyond.

Victory!

As Wilberforce aged, he continued to persist: every year a speech, every year another vote, every year defeat. Finally, he was unable to continue for health reasons, and he retired to his home in London. While he was struggling with what would be his final illness, a great discussion of the subject of slavery was once again before the House of Commons. A motion was made to end slavery *in all* of the colonies of Great Britain around the world; the vote was cast; the motion passed.

There was a great outcry of joy among all

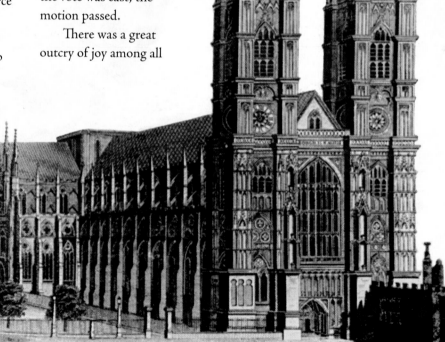

74

of those who had worked with Wilberforce for so long to end slavery. They sent a runner to Wilberforce's home to tell him before he died that at last his great cause had been won. Of course, he rejoiced in the Lord that this had happened and that a lifetime of effort had succeeded.

Let me point out to you that Great Britain ended slavery without a civil war, due to his tremendous drive and commitment to a totally unpopular cause. In England, slavery wasn't unpopular in one-half of the country and popular in the other half — it was popular *everywhere*. There was hardly a businessman in England that didn't have some way of making money off of slavery, and so it was resisted everywhere. In spite of that, they never had a civil war, and slavery ended.

Seven hundred thousand slaves were manumitted when that decision was made in the British Parliament. They were released from their chains; they were delivered from their slavery by the efforts of a little man that people compared to a "shrimp." That took place not too many years before the shot was heard at Fort Sumter, and the Civil War began in America. It took a war in this country to bring an end to slavery.

When Wilberforce died, his body was interred at Westminster Abbey. There he was buried with the greats of that nation.

Enslaved to Sin

Only Christ can set the prisoner free. I don't know about you, but I have given my life, thus far, to trying to bring about the remission of sin and the deliverance from the chains and tyranny of it.

"My walk, I am sensible, is a public one; my business is in the world; and I must mix in assemblies of men, or quit the post which Providence seems to have assigned me."
— William Wilberforce

This is one phase of that effort. We have ten ministries, and the Center for Christian Statesmanship is just one phase of that, which involves, also, getting the government out of the way. I don't think the government can save anyone. However, I do believe the government can get out of the way and let the Church be the Church in all of America.

There are those who have been working assiduously to remove the influence of Christ from the public square in every way they can. What we hope will happen as our government becomes more amenable to the great virtues that made this country, the nation that we know and love, is that there will be a great revival in this country and that increasing numbers of people will be saved. We can talk about the ills of this country, and I often have — so have you — and there are many. They are on the surface to see; they are on the front pages of the newspaper daily. What you don't see is that beneath the surface, there is something going on. There is a great increase in the number of real Christians in America.

Wilberforce wrote a book that contrasted the nominal Christianity of the day with *real* Christianity, and it was published in 20 editions! That was back in the 1700s. His book *Real Christianity* is still being published today.

EDITOR'S NOTE:
This is the abridged sermon, as delivered by Dr. D. James Kennedy at the Center for Christian Statesmanship's Tenth Anniversary Gala, September 28, 2005. Reprinted by permission.
© 2005 D. James Kennedy

The great reformer William Wilberforce was born August 24, 1759, to Elizabeth and Robert Wilberforce. His father and his grandfather, who was young William's namesake, were merchants in Hull, a major seaport of the day. The family acquired their wealth through their trade in the Baltic Sea.

Brought up in a lavish environment of culture, taste, and society, Wilberforce enjoyed a happy, privileged childhood. He resided with his parents in an impressive Jacobean mansion on High Street in Hull, in the county Yorkshire along the River Humber. Visiting there today, one can imagine the young William playing inside magnificent walled gardens, which inspired his lifelong love of nature.

Young Wilberforce

The only son and heir of his father, Wilberforce was provided with a distinguished education at Hull Grammar School. Already showing signs of being a great orator, Wilberforce impressed his tutor, Isaac Milner, who asked his young pupil to stand on a table and read aloud for his classmates so they could observe his polished elocution. Unlike many fathers of the day, Robert Wilberforce was very close to his young son and sent him to day school

for two years in order to keep the boy at home. A family friend, who became ill while in their home, wrote of the young lad, "An unusual thoughtfulness for others marked his youngest childhood. I shall never forget how he would steal into my sickroom, taking off his shoes lest he should disturb me, and with an anxious face look through my curtains to learn if I was better."

At the age of nine, Wilberforce's idyllic childhood ended tragically in 1798 when his older sister and his father died a few months apart. His mother Elizabeth, who was expecting another child, also fell ill. Fearing her death was eminent, Elizabeth sent her young son to live in London with his father's elder brother, also named William, and his wife Hannah at St. James' Place.

These sad circumstances proved fortuitous in the upbringing of Wilberforce, laying the foundation for the later purpose God had planned for his life. His aunt's family, the Thorntons, would later play a major role in the life of Wilberforce as well as his mission in life.

The childless uncle and aunt doted upon their grieving nephew, enrolling him in Putney, a school he once described as "the meanest of character." Wilberforce wrote of his experience: "It was frequented chiefly by the sons of merchants, and they taught therefore everything and nothing." He bore no fondness for his two years spent at Putney, but he was deeply influenced at home by the faith of his aunt and uncle and their evangelical friends.

Wilberforce was a child in the period known as the Great Awakening when a revival swept across England. His guardians were deeply inspired by the sermons of George Whitefield and John Wesley, the founder of Methodism. His aunt Hannah was the sister of Christian activist John Thornton of the wealthy banking family. The Great Awakening paved the way for the two great causes, the abolition of slavery and the return to morality, which Wilberforce would later champion.

Deeply religious, his aunt and uncle were close friends of John Newton, the former slave-ship captain, who penned the legendary hymn, "Amazing Grace." Wilberforce's aunt and uncle took him to the church in Olney, where Newton was now a pastor. Newton also frequently visited their home to "parlor preach." Newton, who was saved and transformed by the great mercy and grace of the Almighty Savior, mesmerized the young Wilberforce with tales of his days at sea as an evil ship captain aboard a slave ship. The passionate preacher made a lasting impact on young William and would later counsel him in his life pursuits.

Enthused over his newfound faith, Wilberforce wrote long letters to his mother. Angered by the religious overtones of her son's letters, his mother discussed the matter with his grandfather, and together they threatened to bring the boy home. "If Billy turns Methodist, he shan't have a sixpence of mine," his

The grand staircase in Wilberforce's home

Wilberforce's house in Hull

and soon he became one of the most sought after young people in the Hull area.

Now enrolled in school at Pocklington, he indulged himself in a life of idleness and pleasure. Although he rarely studied, he continued to excel in his schoolwork. His headmaster Rev. Baskett at Pocklington, formerly a fellow at St. James College, Cambridge, suggested his mother send Wilberforce to Cambridge after he graduated from Pocklington.

By the time Wilberforce enrolled at Cambridge, his family's efforts to cleanse him of his Methodism had not only succeeded, but he had also become a religious

Grandfather Wilberforce declared. Finally, his mother did bring her son home to Hull.

Sadly, Wilberforce wrote of his departure, "I deeply felt the parting, for I loved them as parents." For three years he continued to secretly send anguished letters of his homesickness to his uncle and aunt.

Back at home in Hull, he described his family's efforts to cleanse him of Methodism; "No pains were spared to stifle them." Soon parlor preaching was replaced with socializing — at the theater, lavish balls, and sumptuous suppers at the homes of the local gentry. Before long, Wilberforce had accepted and had even grown to enjoy his new lifestyle. He became known for his charm and singing voice at parties,

Robert Wilberforce

skeptic of weak moral fiber. The recent death of his uncle left him with an enormous fortune and the country home Lauriston House in Wimbledon. Most of his time at Cambridge was spent gambling, drinking, and cavorting. Fortunately for him, he was a very good card player and usually won at these games. Instead of studying, he held court in his room in the evenings where many of his fellow students gathered for supper, games, and stimulating conversation.

When he tried to apply himself at school, even his professors would discourage him, asking, "Why in the world should a man of your fortune trouble himself with fagging study?" However, in his last years at Cambridge he was fueled with ambition when he made friends with the sons of nobility and members of Parliament, including William Pitt, the son of Lord Chatham, Britain's former prime minister, who was being groomed for politics.

Pondering a future in politics, Wilberforce began to apply himself at college. During his last year at Cambridge, he made an important decision not to go into his family's merchant business, but to seek election in Parliament. He began visiting the gallery at Parliament, and became even closer friends with Pitt. By graduation, he was adopted into Pitt's crowd, and he joined several clubs in London, further expanding his social circle, to the delight of his mother. And so the stage for the future of William Wilberforce, the great reformer, was set.[1]

[1] This information was obtained from Jayne Tyler, Keeper of Social History at the Wilberforce House Museum in Hull England. Ms. Tyler graciously gave Kevin Belmonte and me a personal tour and shared the above information with us while we were gathering research for the film, *Amazing Grace*.

"Shall we increase the guilt of which we are now sensible? Shall we continue those practices, which we know to be war with every dictate of justice and humanity? No, Sir; let us no longer be objects of such a reproach. Let us reflect, that at the moment this discussion is going forward, the severest of sufferings are endured in Africa; let us consider the number of ships now sailing from its coast, and the miseries entailed upon the Wretches they are conveying to our Colonies."

William Wilberforce

Obstacles

The perseverance and the obstacles throughout the four decades of Wilberforce's single-minded battle for abolition, first to abolish the slave *trade*, and then to slavery *itself*, coupled with the massive financial interests of the opposition, both personal and national, is remarkable. It seemed utterly unthinkable to the Parliament that they could go without what the plantations of the West Indies provided, such as sugar in their tea. Of great concern were the international politics — how Britain was positioned in relation to the brand new nation of the United States of America, as well as France, Portugal, and Brazil. The opposition also argued that if one nation, like Britain, unilaterally abolished the slave trade, then the power and wealth would be transmitted to the other nations, weakening Britain internationally.

Wilberforce was also the object of public criticism and vicious slander. When Wilberforce won the first victory over the slave trade in February 1807, at the age of 47, John Pollock said, "His achievement brought him a personal moral authority with public and Parliament above any living man."[1] But, as every public person knows, and as Jesus promised,[2] "the best of men will be maligned for the best of actions."

On one occasion in 1820, thirteen years after the first victory, he took an extremely controversial position with regard to Queen Caroline's marital faithfulness and experienced a dramatic public outrage against him. He wrote in his diary July 20, 1820, "What a lesson it is to a man not to set his heart on low popularity when after 40 years disinterested public service, I am believed by the Bulk to be a Hypocritical Rascal. O what a comfort it is to have to fly for refuge to a God of unchangeable truth and love."[3]

Probably the severest criticism he ever received was from a slavery-defending adversary named William Cobett, in August of 1823, who turned Wilberforce's commitment to abolition into a moral liability by claiming that Wilberforce pretended to care for slaves from Africa but cared nothing about the "wage slaves" — the wretched poor of England.

> You seem to have a great affection for the fat and lazy and laughing and singing and dancing Negroes . . . [But] Never have you done one single act in favor of the laborers of this country [a statement Cobett knew to be false]. . . . You make your appeal in Piccadilly, London, amongst those who are wallowing in luxuries, proceeding from the labor of the people. You should have gone to the gravel-pits, and made your appeal to the wretched creatures with bits of sacks around their shoulders, and with hay-bands round their legs; you should have gone to the roadside, and made your appeal to the emaciated, half-dead things who are there cracking stones to make the roads as level as a die for the tax eaters to ride on. What an insult it is, and what an unfeeling, what a cold-blooded hypocrite must he be that can send it forth; what an insult to call upon people under the name of free British laborers; to appeal to them in behalf of Black slaves, when these free British laborers; these poor, mocked, degraded wretches,

A cartoon from 1822 of Wilberforce at the statue of Achilles at Hyde Park Corner making fun of his push for moral reform. Here he is mocked for supposedly trying to have the statue's private parts covered from 10:00 a.m. to dusk.

would be happy to lick the dishes and bowls, out of which the Black slaves have breakfasted, dined, or supped.[4]

But far more painful than any of these criticisms were the heartaches of family life. Every leader knows that almost any external burden is bearable if the family is whole and happy. But when the family is torn, all burdens are doubled. Wilberforce and his wife, Barbara, were very different. "While he was always cheerful, Barbara was often depressed and pessimistic. She finally worried herself into very bad health which lasted the rest of her life." And other women who knew her said she "whined when William was not right beside her."[5]

When his oldest, William, was at Trinity College, Oxford, he fell away from the Christian faith and gave no evidence, as Wilberforce wrote in his, diary of "the great change." He wrote on January 10, 1819, "O that my poor dear William might be led by thy grace, O God." On March 11, he poured out his grief, "Oh my poor William. How strange he can make so miserable those who love him best and whom really he loves. His soft nature makes him the sport of his companions, and the wicked and idle naturally attach themselves like dust and cleave like burrs. I go to pray for him. Alas, could I love my Savior more and serve him, God would hear my prayer and turn his heart."[6]

He got word from Henry Venn that William was not reading for his classes, but was spending his father's allowance foolishly, buying an extra horse. Wilberforce agonized and decided to cut off his allowance, have him suspended from school and put with another family, and not allow him home. "Alas my poor William! How sad to be compelled to banish my eldest son."[7] Even when William finally came back to faith, it grieved Wilberforce that three of his sons became very high-church Anglicans with little respect for the dissenting church that Wilberforce, even as an Anglican, loved so much for its evangelical truth and life.[8]

On top of this family burden came the death of his daughter Barbara. In the autumn of 1821, at 32, she was diagnosed with consumption (tuberculosis). She died five days after Christmas. Wilberforce wrote to a friend, "Oh my dear Friend, it is in such seasons as these that the value of the promises of the Word of God are ascertained both by the dying and the attendant relatives. . . . The assured persuasion of Barbara's happiness has taken away the sting of death."[9] He sounds strong, but the blow shook his remaining strength, and in March of 1822, he wrote to his son, "I am confined by a new malady, the Gout."[10]

The word "new" in that letter signals that Wilberforce labored under some other extraordinary physical handicaps that made his long perseverance in political life all the more remarkable. He wrote in 1788 that his eyes were so bad "[I can scarcely] see how to direct my pen." The humorous side to this was that "he was often shabbily dressed, according to one friend, and his clothes sometimes were put on crookedly because he never looked into a mirror. Since his eyes were too bad to let him see his image clearly, he doesn't bother to look at all!"[11] In fact, there was little humor in his eye disease. In later years, he frequently mentioned the "peculiar complaint of my eyes," that he could not see well enough to read or write during the first hours of the day. "This was a symptom of a slow build-up of morphine poisoning."[12]

This ominous assessment was owing to the fact that from 1788 on, doctors prescribed daily opium pills to Wilberforce to control the debility of his ulcerative colitis. The medicine was viewed in his day as a "pure drug" and it never occurred to any of his enemies to reproach him for his dependence on opium to control his illness.[13] "Yet, effects there must have been," Pollock observes. "Wilberforce certainly grew more untidy, indolent (as he often bemoaned), and absent-minded as his years went on though not yet in old age; it is proof of the strength of his will that he achieved so much under a burden which neither he nor his doctors understood."[14]

In 1812 Wilberforce decided to resign his seat in Yorkshire — not to leave politics, but to take a less demanding seat from a smaller county. He gave his reason as the desire to spend more time with his family. The timing was good, because in the next two years, on top of his colon and eye problems and emerging lung problem, he developed a curvature of the spine. "One shoulder began to slope; and his head fell forward, a little more each year until it rested on his chest unless lifted by conscious movement: he could have looked grotesque were it not for the charm of his face and the smile which hovered about his mouth."[15] For the rest of his life he wore a brace beneath his clothes that most people knew nothing about.[16]

Duke of Wellington

A Key to His Perseverance

As evidenced by the testimonies of many, the key to Wilberforce's perseverance was his child-like, child-loving, self-forgetting joy in Christ as evidenced by the testimonies of many. A Miss Sullivan wrote to a friend about Wilberforce in about 1815: "By the tones of his voice and expression of his countenance he showed that *joy* was the prevailing feature of his own mind, joy springing from entireness of trust in the Savior's merits and from love to God and man. . . . His joy was quite penetrating."[17]

The poet Robert Southey proclaimed, "I never saw any other man who seemed to enjoy such a perpetual serenity and sunshine of spirit. In conversing with him, you feel assured that there is no guile in him; that if ever there was a good man and happy man on earth, he was one."[18] In 1881, Dorothy Wordsworth wrote, "Though shattered in constitution and feeble in body, he is as lively and animated as in the days of his youth."[19] His sense of humor and delight in all that was good was vigorous and unmistakable. In 1824, John Russell gave a speech in the Commons with such wit that Wilberforce "collapsed in helpless laughter."[20]

This playful side made him a favorite of children, as they were favorites of his. His best friend's daughter, Marianne Thornton, said that often "Wilberforce would interrupt his serious talks with her father and romp with her in the lawn. His love for and enjoyment in all children was remarkable."[21] Once, when his own children were playing upstairs and he was frustrated at having misplaced a letter, he heard the great din of children shouting. His guest thought he would be perturbed. Instead, he got a smile on his face and said, "What a blessing to have these dear children! Only think what a relief, amidst other hurries, to hear their voices and know they are well."[22]

He was an unusual father for his day. Most fathers who had the wealth and position he did rarely saw their children. Servants and a governess took care of the children, and they were to be out of sight

James Stephen (1758–1832)
the author of The Memoirs

most of the time. Instead, William insisted on eating as many meals as possible with the children, and he joined in their games. He played marbles and blindman's bluff and ran races with them. In the games, the children treated him like one of them.[23]

Robert Southey visited the house when all the children were there and wrote that he marveled at "the pell-mell, topsy-turvy and chaotic confusion" of the Wilberforce apartments in which the wife sat like Patience on a monument while her husband "frisks about as if every vein in his body were filled with quicksilver."[24] Another visitor in 1816, Joseph John Gurney, a Quaker, stayed a week with Wilberforce and recalled later, "As he walked about the house he was generally humming the tune of a hymn or Psalm, as if he could not contain his pleasurable feelings of thankfulness and devotion."[25]

There was in this child-like love of children and joyful freedom from care a deeply healthy self-forgetfulness. Richard Wellesley, Duke of Wellington, wrote after a meeting with Wilberforce, "You have made me so entirely forget you are a great man by seeming to forget it yourself in all our intercourse."[26] The effect of this self-forgetting joy was another mark of mental and spiritual health, namely, a joyful ability to see all the good in the world instead of being consumed by one's own problems (even when those problems are huge). James Stephen recalled after Wilberforce's death, "Being himself amused and interested by everything, whatever he said became amusing or interesting. . . . His presence was as fatal to dullness as to immorality. His mirth was as irresistible as the first laughter of childhood."[27]

Here was a great key to his perseverance and effectiveness. His presence was "fatal to dullness and immorality." In other words, his indomitable joy moved others to be good and happy. He sustained himself and swayed others by his joy. If a man can rob you of your joy, he can rob you of your usefulness. Wilberforce's joy was indomitable, and therefore he was a compelling Christian and politician all his life.

Hannah More, his wealthy friend and patron of many of his schemes for doing good, said to him, "I declare I think you are serving God by being yourself agreeable . . . to worldly but well-disposed people, who would never be attracted to religion by grave and severe divines, even if such fell in their way."[28] In fact, I think one of the reasons Wilberforce did not like to use the word "Calvinist," though his doctrines seem to line up with what the Whitefield- and Newton-like Calvinists preached, was this very thing: Calvinists had the reputation of being joyless.

A certain Lord Carrington apparently expressed to Wilberforce his mistrust of joy. Wilberforce responded: "My grand objection to the religious system still held by many who declare themselves orthodox Churchmen . . . is, that it tends to render Christianity so much a system of prohibitions rather than of privilege and hopes, and thus the injunction to rejoice, so strongly enforced in the New Testament, is practically neglected, and Religion is made to wear a forbidding and gloomy air and not one of peace and hope and joy."[29]

Here is a clear statement of Wilberforce's conviction that joy is not optional. It is an "injunction . . . strongly enforced in the New Testament." Or, as he says elsewhere, "We can scarcely indeed look into any part of the sacred volume without meeting abundant proofs, that it is the religion of the Affections which God particularly requires. . . . Joy . . . is enjoined on us as our bounden duty and commended to us as our acceptable worship. . . . A cold . . . unfeeling heart is represented as highly criminal."[30]

So for Wilberforce, joy was both a means of survival and perseverance on the one hand, and a deep act of submission and obedience and worship on the other hand. Joy in Christ was commanded. And joy in Christ was the only way to flourish fruitfully through decades of temporary defeat. "Never were there times," he wrote, "which inculcated more forcibly than those in which we live, the wisdom of seeking happiness beyond the reach of human vicissitudes."[31]

The word "seeking" is important. It is not as though Wilberforce succeeded perfectly in "attaining" the fullest measure of joy. There were great battles in the soul as well as in Parliament. For example, in March of 1788, after a serious struggle with colitis, he seemed to enter into a "dark night of the soul." "Corrupt imaginations are perpetually rising in my mind and innumerable fears close to me in on every side. . . ."[32] We get a glimpse of how he fought for joy in these times from what he wrote in his notebook of prayers, "Lord, thou knowest that no strength, wisdom or contrivance of human power can signify, or relieve me. It is in thy power alone to deliver me. I fly to thee for succor and support, O Lord let it come speedily; give me full proof of thy Almighty power; I am in great troubles, insurmountable by me; but to thee slight and inconsiderable; look upon me O Lord with compassion and mercy, and restore me to rest, quietness, and comfort, in the world, or in another by removing me hence into a state of peace and happiness. Amen."[33]

Less devastating than "the dark night" were the recurrent disappointments with his personal failures. But even as we read his self-indictments we hear the hope of victory that sustained him and restored him to joy again and again. For example, on January 13, 1798, he wrote in his diary, "Three or four times have I most grievously broke my resolutions since I last took up my pen alas! alas! how miserable a wretch am I! How infatuated, how dead to every better feeling yet . . . yet . . . yet . . . may I, Oh God, be enabled to repent and turn to thee with my whole heart, I am

John Wesley's Letter to William Wilberforce

EDITOR'S NOTE: *William Wilberforce was converted through John Wesley's ministry. The last letter Wesley wrote on his deathbed was a letter of encouragement to Wilberforce.*[35]

Balam, February 24, 1791

Dear Sir:

Unless the divine power has raised you up to be as *Athanasius contra mundum*, I see not how you can go through your glorious enterprise in opposing that execrable villainy which is the scandal of religion, of England, and of human nature. Unless God has raised you up for this very thing, you will be worn out by the opposition of men and devils. But if God be for you, who can be against you? Are all of them together stronger than God? O be not weary of well doing! Go on, in the name of God and in the power of his might, till even American slavery (the vilest that ever saw the sun) shall vanish away before it.

Reading this morning a tract wrote by a poor African, I was particularly struck by that circumstance that a man who has a black skin, being wronged or outraged by a white man, can have no redress; it being a "law" in our colonies that the oath of a black against a white goes for nothing. What villainy is this?

That he who has guided you from youth up may continue to strengthen you in this and all things, is the prayer of, dear sir,

Your affectionate servant,
John Wesley

Wesley writing his last letter to Wilberforce

now flying from thee. Thou hast been above all measure gracious and forgiving. . . ."[34] Therefore, when we say his happiness was unshakable and undefeatable because it was beyond the reach of human vicissitudes, we don't mean it was beyond struggle; we mean it reasserted itself in and after every tumult in society of in the soul.

The Foundation for Joy

The child-like and indomitable joy of William Wilberforce was the key to his perseverance in the life-long cause of abolition and the pursuit of justice.

The main burden of Wilberforce's book, *A Practical View of Christianity*, is to show that true Christianity, which consists in these new, indomitable spiritual affections for Christ, is rooted in the great doctrines of the Bible about sin and Christ and faith. "Let him then who would abound and grow in this Christian principle, be much conversant with the great doctrines of the Gospel."[36] More specifically, he says, "If we would . . . rejoice in [Christ] as triumphantly as the first Christians did; we must learn, like them to repose our entire trust in Him and to adopt the language of the apostle, 'God forbid that I should glory, save in the cross of Jesus Christ' (Gal. 6:14), 'who of God is made unto us wisdom and righteousness, and sanctification, and redemption'" (1 Cor. 1:30).[37]

In other words, the joy that triumphs over all obstacles and perseveres to the end in the battle for justice is centrally rooted in the doctrine of justification by faith. Wilberforce says that all the spiritual and practical errors of the nominal Christians of his age — the lack of true religious affections and moral reformation — resulted from the mistaken conception entertained of the fundamental principles of Christianity. They consider not that Christianity is scheme "for justifying *the ungodly*" (Rom. 4:5), by Christ's dying for them "*when yet sinners*" (Rom. 5:6–8), a scheme "for reconciling us to God — *when enemies*" (Rom. 5:10); and for making the fruits of holiness *the effects, not the cause*, of our being justified and reconciled.[38]

William Wilberforce

From the beginning of his Christian life in 1785 until he died in 1833, Wilberforce lived off the "great doctrines of the gospel," especially the doctrine of justification by faith alone based on the blood and righteousness of Jesus Christ. This is where he fed his joy; and the joy of the Lord became his strength (Neh. 8:10). In this strength he pressed on in the cause of abolishing the slave trade until he had the victory.

Therefore, in all zeal for racial harmony and the rebuilding of white evangelical and black culture, let us not forget these lessons: Never minimize the central place of God-centered, Christ-exalting doctrine; labor to be indomitably joyful in all that God is for us in Christ by trusting his great finished work; and never be idle in doing good — that men may see your good deeds and give glory to your Father who is in heaven (Matt. 5:16).

EDITOR'S NOTE:
By John Piper. ©Desiring God. Website: www.desiringGod.org. Email: mail@desiringGod.org. Toll Free: 888.346.470. Dr. Piper is also the author of Amazing Grace in the Life of William Wilberforce, which will be released by Crossway in January 2007. This article is used by permission.

1   John Pollock, *Wilberforce* (London: Constable and Company, 1977), p. 215. Wilberforce's own assessment of the resulting moral authority was this (written in a letter March 3, 1807): "The authority which the great principles of justice and humanity have received will be productive of benefit in all shapes and directions."

2   "If they have called the master of the house Beelzebul, how much more will they malign those of his household" (Matt. 10:25).

3   Betty Steele Everett, *Freedom Fighter: The Story of William Wilberforce* (Fort Washington, PA: Christian Literature Crusade, 1994); Pollock, *Wilberforce*, p. 276.

4   Ibid. p. 287.

5   Everett, *Freedom Fighter*, p. 64–65.

6   Pollock, *Wilberforce*, p. 267.

7   Ibid., p. 268. From the diary, April 11, 1819.

8   The official biography written by his sons is defective in portraying Wilberforce in a false light as opposed to dissenters, when in fact some of his best friends and spiritual counselors were among their number. After Wilberforce's death three of his sons became Roman Catholic.

9   Ibid., p. 280.

10   Ibid.

11   Everett, *Freedom Fighter*, p. 69.

12   Ibid., p. 81.

13   Ibid. See p. 79–81 for a full discussion of the place of opium in his life and culture. "Wilberforce resisted the craving and only raised his dosage suddenly when there were severe bowel complaints. In April 1818, 30 years after the first prescription, Wilberforce noted in his diary, "It's still as it has long been, a pill three times a day (after breakfast, after tea, and bedtime) each of four grains. Twelve grains daily is a good but not outstanding dose and very far from addiction after such a length of time."

14   Ibid., p. 81.

15   Ibid., p. 234.

16   "He was obliged to wear 'a steel girdle cased in leather and an additional part to support the arms. . . . It must be handled carefully, the steel being so elastic as to be easily broken.' He took a spare one ('wrapped up for decency's sake in a towel') wherever he stayed; the fact that he lived in a steel frame for his last 15 or 18 years might have remained unknown had he not left behind at the Lord Calthorpe's Suffolk home, Ampton Hall, the more comfortable of the two. 'How gracious is God,' Wilberforce remarked in the letter asking for its return, 'in giving us such mitigations and helps for our infirmities.'" Ibid., p. 233–234.

17   Ibid., p. 152.

18   William Jay, The *Autobiography of William Jay*, edited by George Redford and John Angell James (Edinburgh: The Banner of Truth Trust, 1974, original, 1854), p. 317.

19   Pollock, *Wilberforce*, p. 267.

20   Ibid., p. 289

21   Ibid., p. 183.

22   Ibid., p. 232.

23   Everett, *Freedom Fighter*, p. 70.

24   Pollock, *Wilberforce*, p. 267.

25   Ibid., p. 261.

26   Ibid., p. 236.

27   Ibid., p. 185.

28   Ibid., p. 119.

29   Ibid., p. 46.

30   Ibid., p. 45–46.

31   Ibid., p. 239.

32   Ibid., p. 82.

33   Ibid., p. 81–82.

34   Ibid., p. 150. He confesses again after a sarcastic rejoinder in the Commons, "In what a fermentation of spirits was I on the night of answering Courtenay. How jealous of character and greedy of applause. Alas, alas! Create in me a clean heart O God and renew a right spirit within me" (p. 167).

35   A.H. Hyde, *The Story of Methodism Throughout the World, from the Beginning to the Present Time* (Springfield, MA: Wiley & Co., 1889).
     W.B. Daniels, *The Illustrated History of Methodism in Great Britain, America, and Australia* (New York: Methodist Book Concern, 1884).

36   Wilberforce, *A Practical View of Christianity*, p. 170.

37   Ibid., p. 66.

38   Ibid., p. 64.

Wilberforce had a brief romance with a Miss Hammond, a sister-in-law of the speaker of the House, Henry Addington, in 1789. Although he was in love, he wrote, "It is very likely that I shall never change my condition; nor do I feel solicitous whether I do or not."[1] Wilberforce explained the "difference of views and Plans for life" between himself and "Miss H." were such that "they could not have been happy together."[2] Deciding against marriage, he fully committed himself to God's great call on his life.

In 1796, when his closest friend, Henry Thornton, married his childhood friend, Marianne Sykes, Wilberforce began to long for a wife and family himself. He wrote a friend, quoting his favorite Cowper, that he wished "not to finish my journey alone."[3]

After he shared his sudden longings for a wife with his friend, Thomas Babington, Wilberforce listened intently as Babington described a beautiful young woman who had become an ardent evangelical Christian . . . Barbara Ann Spooner. She was the eldest daughter of evangelical Isaac Spooner, Esquire of Elmdon House, Warwickshire.

At Babington's urging, Barbara wrote to William Wilberforce. Utterly charmed by her letter, Wilberforce spoke to his friend Babington again concerning the young woman, and made arrangements to meet her two days later.

The meeting proved to be love at first sight for both of them. After a whirlwind courtship of a mere eight days, Wilberforce proposed to Barbara by letter. She wrote back that same evening accepting his proposal of marriage. Upon receiving the letter, Wilberforce was so excited that he could hardly sleep!

"Above all the women I know, Barbara is qualified in all respects to make me a good wife," he wrote to his friend Matthew Montagu.[4] Wilberforce wrote of his future bride in his diary: "I believe her to be a real Christian, affectionate, sensible, rational in habits, moderate in desires and pursuits, capable of bearing prosperity without intoxication, and adversity without complaining."[5] Outstanding characteristics for a wife!

A mere two weeks after they first met, William Wilberforce married Barbara Ann Spooner on May 30, 1770. He was 38-years-old, and she was 20. From 1792 until his marriage, Wilberforce had occupied apartments in Henry Thornton's house at Battersea Rise. After his marriage, he took his bride to live at Broomfield, a house on the southwest side of Clapham Common, on the Thornton estate near Henry and Marianne Thornton's home. In a letter to his brother-in-law, James Stevens, who was married to one of his sisters, Wilberforce wrote. "A more tender, excellent wife no man ever received (as a) gift from the Lord."[6]

It was apparent to their friends and family how much in love the couple was. One of their first visits was to the home of Hannah More, who remarked that she had "never seen an honest gentleman more desperately in love." But not all of Wilberforce's friends were impressed with his choice of a wife, though one friend did note, "No one would have known how much of an angel was in him if they had not seen his behaviour to one whose tastes must have tried his patience so much."[7]

Others described Barbara Ann Spooner as slow, whiny, fussy, and altogether a poor housekeeper. What Wilberforce described as her *excessive affection,* friends called *"over-protectiveness"!* Yet this "over-protectiveness" is perhaps what helped to preserve her husband's life.[8]

Mrs. Wilberforce affectionately called her beloved husband "Wilby." Within ten years of marriage, she bore him four boys and two girls. With a house filled with animals of every description, including a tame hare, the couple raised their children in a home that was described by several friends as zoo-like. Although their home life appeared chaotic to others, their household was also comfortable and loving. The couple never allowed anything to get in the way of their family life. Picnics were a regular occurrence and festive scenes were commonplace in the Wilberforce home, for he loved his children's "Holy Day amusements."[9]

Marianne Thorton, the eldest daughter of their friends Henry and Marianne Thornton, recalled, "I know one of my first lessons was I must never disturb Papa when he was talking or reading, but no such prohibition existed with Mr. Wilberforce. His love for and enjoyment in all children was remarkable."[10]

Barbara constantly doted on her husband, often to the detriment of their guests. Although a few of their guests complained, Wilberforce never appeared to mind or even notice. His wife was obviously the perfect companion for him.

As their children left home to marry, the couple delighted in them as adults, and their spouses, as well. They adored their grandchildren. As Jesus said, "the storms will come," and their life was no exception. Having lost one of their daughters and a grandchild, their hearts were filled with sorrow, but they leaned heavily on their faith to survive the tragedies, finding solace in the Lord, as well as one another.

On March 16, 1824, Wilberforce again spoke vigorously against slavery, but three days later, he became seriously ill. He made one more speech upon the same topic, and then had another attack, which made his retirement necessary in March 1825. He and his wife left London and bought 140 acres at Highwood Hill, near Mill Hill, where they retired. Living quietly, they enjoyed their garden and frequent visits by their family and friends.

Barbara Spooner

In 1831, with their enormous fortune depleted by their generosity and somewhat by the continuing financial woes of their eldest son, the Wilberforces were no longer able to afford Highwood Hill and were forced to leave. Although the details are not known, a group of people, including his old political opponent, Lord Fitzwilliam, made offers which "would have at once restored his fortune."

Wilberforce, however, refused their offers, choosing instead to reside happily between the homes of his two sons, Robert, vicar of East Farleigh in Kent, and Samuel, vicar of Brighstone or Brixton in the Isle of Wight. Once again tragedy struck when his second daughter died soon afterward. In May 1833, the couple traveled to Bath after Wilberforce had an attack of influenza. His strength continued to decline, and in July he was moved to London. While there, he heard of the second reading of the bill for the abolition of slavery, and just days before he died, his friends came to his home to tell him the bill to abolish slavery throughout the British Empire had passed at last!

Three days before he died, he remarked, "I do declare, that the delight I have in feeling that there are few people whose hearts are really attached to me, is the very highest I have in this world. What more could any wish at the close of life, than to be attended by his own children, and his own wife, and all treating him with such uniform kindness and affection?"[11]

1. John Pollock, *Wilberforce*, (London: John Constable, 1977) p. 95.
2. Ibid, p. 94.
3. Line 10 of Cowper's poem, *Verses*.
4. John Pollock, *Wilberforce*, (London: John Constable, 1977) p. 158.
5. Ibid. p. 215.
6. Robert Isaac and Samuel Wilberforce, *The Life of William Wilberforce*, vol. 3, (London, John Murray, 1838). p. 529.
7. Betty Steele Everett, *Freedom Fighter: The Story of William Wilberforce* (Fort Washington, PA: Christian Literature Crusade, 1994). pp. 64-65.
8. Ibid, p. 64-65.
9. Robert Isaac and Samuel Wilberforce, *The Life of William Wilberforce*, vol. 5, (London, John Murray, 1838) p. 225.
10. John Pollock, *Wilberforce*, (London: John Constable, 1977) P. 183.
11. Ibid, p. 371 At the time of his death on July 29, 1833, William Wilberforce had been blissfully married to his beloved wife Barbara for 36 years.

In 1780, a young man stepped onto the stage of history who was destined to make a greater impact upon the world humanitarian scene than any other individual either before or since. He was William Wilberforce, newly elected Member of Parliament for Hull in East Yorkshire.

It had only been four years since the 13 British colonies in America had declared independence from England and formed the United States of America. Relationships across the Atlantic were still tense. The American navy was patrolling the Atlantic, harassing Britain's trade with the Caribbean, preventing ships from getting through to British ports. France and Spain were fighting Britain on land and sea, and French ships were seriously disrupting Britain's trade and colonial ambitions in India. These actions were causing shortages of basic foods in England that led to increasing unrest among the poor, and "bread riots" in a number of cities.

In fact, England was at war with half the world. Her boast to be "Mistress of the Seas" was not only being challenged by America, France, and Spain, but also by Russia, Prussia, Holland, and the Scandinavian nations who had combined their diplomatic and naval forces in what was known as the "Armed Neutrality of the North" actively to defend the rights of neutrals, thus further isolating the British. Even in Ireland, for the first and only time in history, Protestants and Catholics united to

Cambridge

overthrow the system by which their common interests were sacrificed to that of England.

At the same time, clouds of revolution were gathering over France that were soon to fill the streets of Paris with blood as howling mobs gathered around the guillotine to watch the daily spectacle of public executions. The British aristocracy trembled as these events unfolded, fearing that the violence would spill over into London.

It was not a good time to become a politician, especially for a man with a mission! But Wilberforce had not yet discovered his mission. He was still a raw youth fresh from Cambridge University where he had indulged in all the frivolous pastimes of his day among the over-privileged young men from rich families. At Cambridge, he had become close friends with William Pitt (the Younger), who in 1783 became Britain's youngest-ever prime minister and set about transforming Britain's fortunes by curbing the power of King George III whose stupidity, arrogance, and personal ambition had brought about such intense international opposition and unrest at home.

Wilberforce was highly gifted as a speaker with a ready wit and was much sought-after as a partygoer and popular guest at fashionable gatherings in the homes of the rich and famous. He was often at the court of King George at the invitation of the Prince of Wales and was already regarded as an eloquent and entertaining speaker in the House of Commons with many influential friends in both Houses of Parliament.

Even before his conversion experience that led to his becoming an "enthusiastic" Christian, so abhorred by his mother, his social conscience was stirred. He once participated in a card game at a gaming table when he saw a young man lose a fortune and ruin his life. He vowed then never again to take part in gambling. He kept his vow and later campaigned vigorously on a wide range of moral reforms, including the abolition of dueling and cruel sports such as bear bating and pit-bull and cock fighting, which led to the founding of the Royal Society for the Prevention of Cruelty to Animals (RSPCA).

This was one of some 80 philanthropic and missionary societies formed by Wilberforce and members of the "Clapham" group of Christians (so named because many lived around Clapham Common in South London). The best known of these societies are the London Missionary Society, the Church Missionary Society, the Sunday School Union, and the Bible Society.

But they also formed many philanthropic societies such as the Society for Bettering the Condition and Increasing the Comforts of the Poor, the Friendly Female Society for the Relief of Poor, Infirm, Aged Widows, and Single Women, of Good Character, who have Seen Better Days.

Despite his deep concern for the poor and the powerless, and his renowned philanthropy, Wilberforce did not renounce his birthright and go to live among the poor. He used his position in society and his faith to bring Christian principles into the social and political arenas.

He recognized that if he was to achieve the social reforms he longed to see he had to use the existing power structures. He believed that God had put him into his position in life specifically to use his influence on behalf of the poor and powerless.

Wilberforce became a tireless campaigner for the abolition of slavery, raising the subject in Parliament year after year and enduring sustained ridicule and bitter opposition. But he was also deeply concerned with the moral and spiritual state of the nation. He founded "The Society for the Suppression of Vice," which was not, as his detractors suggested, primarily aimed at curbing the pastimes of the poor. His chief concern was with vice among the ruling classes.

He was deeply committed to changing the lifestyles and values of the rich and powerful. Recognizing that with fear of the French Revolution spreading across the channel political reform would not happen quickly, Wilberforce set himself to use his wit and social influence to win the hearts of those who had the power to bring about social change. He believed that this would only come about through

> *"God has set before me two great objects, the suppression of the slave trade and the reformation of manners."*
> *— William Wilberforce*

commitment to Christ and a life-changing spiritual experience such as he himself had experienced.

Wilberforce longed to see the fashionable pursuits of the idle rich transformed. So he stated that his personal ambition was "To Make Goodness Fashionable." The measure of his success in changing the mindset of the privileged families of his day can be judged from the fact that the abolition of the slave trade and the abolition of the institution of slavery, as well as many acts of social reformation, were actually achieved under the old parliamentary system long before the franchise was granted to all men and women in Britain. Wilberforce recognized that it is only changed men and women who can bring about any real transformation of society for the common good. He also knew from personal experience that the power to change lives only came through the gospel and a personal relationship with Jesus.

EDITOR'S NOTE:

The Rev. Dr. Clifford Hill is author of more than 30 books and countless magazine, journal, and newspaper articles. Academically, he is both a sociologist and a theologian. His pastoral ministry has been in inner-city areas of London where he has ministered among a multicultural population and been widely recognized as a writer and lecturer on community relationships. He is a member of the Parliamentary Family and Child Protection Group. He founded the Family Matters Institute and remains its research director. Together with his wife, Monica, he leads the Centre for Contemporary Ministry at Moggerhanger Park, the famous country house of the Thornton family, cousins of William Wilberforce, and linked to the Clapham Sect. Their work today is widely recognized as having a similar prophetic nature through the application of the gospel to the great social issues of the day.

A poor family living in the streets of London

> "History has had no other such 'brotherhood of Christian politicians.' By the liberality of their minds no less than of their purses, by their chosen cause, their concerted labors . . . . their persistent and triumphant campaigns, they made a permanent difference to the history, not only of England, but of the modern world."
> – E.M. Howse, *(speaking of the Clapham circle)*

When after much struggle and effort, the abolition bill passed in 1807, William Wilberforce said to his friend Henry Thornton, "Well, Henry, what shall we abolish next?"

The comment illustrates Wilberforce's innate optimism, but the "we" also reveals something. Though he was probably the greatest social reformer of the 1800s, he never worked alone.

When he was converted to evangelical faith in 1785, Wilberforce soon found himself at the center of a group of well-connected and well-heeled individuals. This group, called the Clapham Sect, combined their considerable talents, religious zeal, and optimism in a concerted campaign of national reform. And in large measure, they succeeded.

Here are some of the leading members and what they accomplished as individuals and as a group.

Henry Thornton (1760–1815)
Financial genius

Whenever the Clapham friends championed a new cause, and a society organized to carry it out, Henry Thornton was the one who gave practical business advice and financial support. He was almost sure to be asked to be the treasurer.

After his conversion, Wilberforce had retreated to the mansion of Henry's father, John Thornton, who lived in Clapham. Wilberforce soon became fast friends with Henry. Henry purchased his own house at Clapham in 1792, and he and Wilberforce lived there together as bachelors for five years. Later, when each had married and established his family, they lived as neighbors on the same estate. It was around Wilberforce and Thornton that the "sect" gradually formed.

Henry, like his father, was a highly successful merchant banker. He had a superb mind for abstract economics, and his business savvy was matched by a liberal generosity. He gave away six-sevenths of his income before he was married and more than a third of it afterward. Probably his greatest personal efforts were expended in directing the affairs of the Sierra Leone Company, a Clapham-inspired enterprise to establish a colony of freed slaves in West Africa.

Thornton was a Member of Parliament for many years, but he never neglected his domestic duties. He conducted regular family worship, and a volume of his family prayers was published after his death.

ARISTOCRATIC ACTIVISTS BY BRUCE HINDMARSH

the early efforts against slavery and helped recruit Wilberforce to the cause.

When Wilberforce was still a child, without any legal training, Sharp had single-handedly overturned the legal opinion of the majority of the most eminent judges in England. Sharp happened upon a slave in London who had been cruelly beaten and abandoned by his West Indian master. Sharp took up the slave's case and achieved, in this case and others, many legal precedents, including the famous 1772 ruling which essentially declared that any slave who set foot in English territory had become free.

Sharp had his share of eccentricities. He rose at dawn to sing psalms in Hebrew to the accompaniment of his harp. He was also keenly interested in the prophetic parts of Scripture. He once gained an audience with the prominent statesman Charles Fox and proceeded to explain to him why Napoleon should be identified with the "little horn" in the book of Daniel.

His political views were more radical than those of most Claphamites, but with them he ardently supported many religious and philanthropic causes. The Sierra Leone experiment was begun at his initiative. He was also one of the founders of the Sunday School Society, the Bible Society, and the Society for Promoting the Conversion of Jews.

Granville Sharp (1735–1813)
Self-taught radical

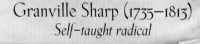

Unlike most of his younger friends at Clapham, Granville Sharp had no inherited wealth and had to work to support himself. But work seemed to come easy to Sharp. While working away at law, he taught himself Hebrew so he could defend Christianity to a Jew, and then Greek, to oppose an infidel skeptic.

Sharp was older than most of the other associates of Wilberforce and more loosely associated with Clapham. But he had pioneered in

John Venn (1759–1813)
Addicted to doing good

John Venn once lamented that a drawback of entering heaven might be the lost opportunities to do good: "There will be no sick to visit, no naked to clothe, no afflicted to relieve, no weak to succor, no faint to encourage, nor corrupt to rebuke or profligate to reclaim."

In 1792, through the patronage of John Thornton, Venn became rector of the parish church in Clapham. He quickly became a spiritual guide to the group, joined in their deliberations, and even led several causes.

Venn set up one of the first organized systems of parish visitation, conducted confirmation classes, and formed the Society for Bettering the Conditions of the Poor. With friends, he financially supported six local schools and took pride that every child in Clapham could receive a free education — an unusual achievement in that day. He saw to it that the parish was vaccinated against smallpox, having his own family vaccinated first as an example.

On the national scene, Venn was the prime mover behind the Church Missionary Society. As founding chairman in 1799, he set it on its influential course as a thoroughly Anglican and evangelical enterprise in foreign missions.

Hannah More (1745–1833)
"Petticoat Bishop"

Because of Hannah More's determined religious activism, one of her opponents once called her "a bishop in petticoats."

Although she lived far from Clapham, in Somerset, More had the closest of links with Wilberforce, Thornton, and their friends. As a young woman, More moved in some of the most fashionable intellectual circles in London, and included the actor David Garrick and Samuel Johnson among her friends. She soon earned a reputation as a successful poet and playwright. After becoming a "serious" Christian in the 1780s, she sought to win her high society friends to her views. She took pen in hand, and her *Thoughts on the Manners of the Great* (1788) became a best seller.

Yet More's most significant work was as an educator and writer on behalf of the lower classes. Prompted by Wilberforce, she and her sister began to work among the poor in the Mendip Hills, south of Bristol. With financial help from Thornton, she soon had over 500 children organized in schools across an area of some 75 square miles. This became the most well-known venture in religious and popular education supported by the Clapham Sect.

More believed the laboring classes needed inexpensive and edifying material to read (among other reasons, so they would not become engrossed in irreligious and politically inflammatory tracts). So she wrote a series of *Cheap Repository Tracts*, which sold at a penny or half-penny a piece and were subsidized by Thornton. Within a year, over two million had been sold.

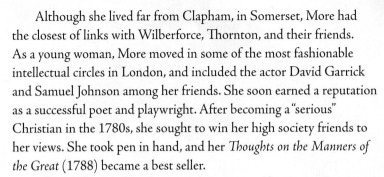

Zacharay Macaulay (1768–1838)
Walking encyclopedia

If any of the Clapham Sect were in doubt about a fact or figure, they used to say, "Look it up in Macaulay." Such was Zacharay Macaulay's reputation for doing research.

Macaulay, as an estate manager in the West Indies, quickly became disgusted

Letter from Wilberforce to Macaulay

with Jamaican slavery. He returned to England in 1792 — only to be selected as the Clapham choice to turn around the fortunes of Sierra Leone. For six years as governor, his administration was plagued by threats of insurrection, harassment by slave-trading interests, and marauding French squadrons before he could bring some order and prosperity to the colony.

He did not seek the most comfortable means to return to England. He somehow talked his way onto a slave ship — to collect eyewitness evidence of the horrific conditions of the Middle Passage from Africa to the West Indies.

In England, Macaulay became a one-man research department for all Clapham causes, and especially for the cause of abolition. With an almost photographic memory, he tirelessly gathered facts, sifted evidence, digested parliamentary papers, and submitted all to powerful analysis. It became a dictum that Macaulay could be quoted verbatim on the floor of the House of Commons without fear of contradiction.

His energies were not exhausted by the antislavery cause. He was the first major editor of the influential *Christian Observer*, which began in 1802 and quickly became the chief organ of Anglican evangelical piety. He was a member of 23 philanthropic and religious societies and on the governing committee of nine.

Democratic Paternalists

The list of influential Claphamites could easily be expanded to include James Stephen, Charles Grant, and John Shore. There was also the indefatigable Thomas Clarkson, one of the key, if forgotten, British abolitionists. He once searched systematically through every ship in England, port after port, in order to find a sailor whom he thought could provide evidence against slavery. (Clarkson found him in the 57th ship.) At Cambridge, there was the knot of students and clergy who surrounded the famous preacher Charles Simeon. They embodied the Clapham Sect's attempt to "evangelize" the Church of England from within.

In spite of the profusion of good people and good works, the Clapham Sect has received criticism, some of it just. To be sure, they were paternalists. Hannah More once said of her poor students, "They have so little common sense, and so little sensibility, that we are obliged to beat into their heads continually the good we are doing to them."

From *The Fight Against Slavery* by Terrence Brady

A poster advertising Sierra Leone, a West African colony the Clapham Sect established for former slaves

Aghast at the irreligion and violence of the French Revolution, the well-to-do at Clapham abhorred many democratic reforms. They supported several repressive measures designed to stave off revolution by keeping political agitators in check — including the Peterloo Massacre in 1819, a violent breakup of a mass meeting about parliamentary reform in which 11 people died.

The Clapham Sect has also been criticized for being more concerned for moral reform among the poor than the rich. One critic said Wilberforce's Society for the Suppression of Vice should be renamed "The Society for the Suppression of Vice among Those with Less Than £500 a Year."

Yet the views of the Clapham Sect were more liberal than was typical for people of their station. Wilberforce often rebuked the sins of the rich and powerful. His friendship with William Pitt, the prime minister, was strained by Wilberforce's public denunciation of dueling (a "sin" of the aristocratic class) in the wake of Pitt's well-known duel with a political enemy.

Moreover, their religious and humanitarian ideals helped bring about a more egalitarian society. The message of salvation for all, the rhetoric of antislavery, and the call for individual responsibility helped move England toward democratic reforms.

The Clapham Sect pioneered techniques of mobilizing public opinion that have become commonplace in democracies. They exploited the media outlets of the day: lectures, billboards, newspapers, and pamphlets. They made effective use of voluntary societies and unprecedented use of petitions to exert public pressure on Parliament.

Wilberforce and his colleagues were remarkably shrewd and skilled in tactical politics, that is, "networking." Nobody could glad-hand at a dinner party like Wilberforce. While keeping a reputation for unsullied integrity, and establishing their independence from vested interests and partisan loyalties, the "Saints" happily cooperated where they could and built limited coalitions. They once noted they were happy to work with the celebrated orator Richard Sheridan, "whether [he was] drunk or sober."

The Wilberforce Sect

If Wilberforce never worked alone, the Clapham Sect couldn't work without Wilberforce. When Wilberforce died in 1833, the group lost its animating center. The causes he and his friends had championed would go on, and the moral and spiritual influence they exerted would continue to be felt, but the Clapham Sect would be no more. It was a phenomenon of one generation. This was a "sect" that gathered less around Clapham than it did around Wilberforce himself.

EDITOR'S NOTE:
Bruce Hindmarsh is a visiting research fellow at Oxford University and author of John Newton and the English Evangelical Tradition *(Oxford University Press, 1996). This article is used by permission. From* Christian History, *Issue 53 (Vol. XVI, No1).*

Most of the facts are not in dispute. He was the son of a prime minister. He entered Cambridge at age 14. He seemed to have a preternatural understanding of the game politicians play. He was, and will likely remain, the youngest prime minister Britain has ever seen. To say that he was a gifted orator is to indulge in understatement. When he gave his first speech in Parliament at the well-cultivated age of 23, the House of Commons was put on notice that Pitt the Younger, as he was called, was a force of his own. He never married, was addicted to port and, in the end, led Parliament for almost 20 years. These things are not debated. What has intrigued students of history for the two centuries since his death is the question of William Pitt's legacy, his ultimate measure as a true leader.

It would be fair to say that William Pitt the Younger got a head start. "Never did a young man find the path to attainment so smoothly paved," writes biographer E. Keble Chatterton.[1] Indeed, as the privileged son of Lord Chatham, William Pitt the Elder, he was immersed in the world of politics practically from the cradle. His childhood frailty and ill health kept him indoors, a tragedy for most boys, except that in his home, the business of running England was at hand.[2] But even these advantages might have been lost on some other child not quite so suited for a life in politics.

Though he lost his first contest for office, his connections secured him another "elected" seat. Such were the times that "without having ever had to visit his constituents, he [took] his place in the House of Commons."[3] Ironically, once in Parliament, Pitt aligned himself to support reforms combating such abuses.

Nevertheless, accounts of his effectiveness as a leader, and certainly as a reformer, vary widely. Admirers argue that when Pitt entered Parliament Britain was in a rut. Disgraced by the loss of her American colonies, debt was mounting and the navy was hemorrhaging sailors from desertion. Hungry for reform, Britain needed a leader to navigate her through the turbulent times ahead. Just miles across the English Channel, the French experiment in freedom and liberty was quickly becoming a thicket of despotism that threatened to cast its seed abroad. The social upheaval of the emerging Industrial Revolution made England fertile soil for a similar fate.[4]

That no such revolution was ever allowed to foment in Britain is, for some, a credit to Pitt's vigilance and firm leadership. It was Pitt's administration, they argue, whose stable continuity protected Britain from anarchy and piloted her through debt and war. In so doing, he was responsible for ushering her into the 19th century poised to become the world's unchallenged superpower.

Still, others maintain that Pitt's achievements are overshadowed by his failure to pursue greater reforms. The British crown may not have been overthrown as the Bourbons were in France, but a stable regime does not guarantee a just society, and for some reformers, Pitt's administration was a disappointment. During his many years in office, most of the harsh domestic conditions that would later keep the Victorian reformers busy (child labor, prisons, criminal law, etc.) remained unchanged. Since he relied more on the king's pleasure for maintaining his position than on the will of the people or even his party, some argue that his longevity in office owed much to his stalwart defense of the status quo.[5] Indeed, even the

THE LEGACY OF WILLIAM PITT THE YOUNGER BY ANDREW PARKER

*Prime Minister
William Pitt
addressing
the House of
Commons*

National Portrait Gallery, London

parliamentary reforms he had sponsored at the start of his career were never heard from again.[6] His distinction as having invented the income tax is particularly dubious.

Then there is slavery. William Pitt's support for the abolitionist cause has been a difficult question for many historians. Publicly and rhetorically, he was a staunch supporter. He lent to the cause his famously splendid and always improvised oratorical performances, including an impassioned speech which is supposed to have concluded just as dawn's rays streamed into the House chamber illuminating his face.[7]

Still, he is thought by some to have been mostly talk — insincere, if not downright duplicitous. Much has been made about his refusal to make the abolition of the slave trade an official position of his government, that is, a matter on which his own administration was prepared to rise or fall. He insisted that his support for abolition was always as a private member of the House and not as its leader.[8]

For 20 years under his government, the abolitionists endeavored to ban the slave trade without success. Then, barely over a year after his death (he died in office in 1806), the bill to end the trade was passed. Some say his intentions were sincere but powerful members in Parliament tied his hands. Others insist those same circumstances persisted after his death, yet with the ascension of a new administration, the abolitionists were able to prevail. Writing in 1838 in the *Edinburgh Review*, "Sir James Stephen, son of [an] abolitionist and himself a distinguished public servant and anti-slavery leader" put it bluntly:

The death of Mr. Pitt approached; an event which the most calm and impartial judgment must now regard as the necessary precursor of the liberation of Africa.... Successful in almost every other Parliamentary conflict, and triumphing over the most formidable antagonist, he had been compelled ... to go to the grave without obliterating that which he himself had denounced as the deepest stain on our national character, and the most enormous guilt recorded in the history of mankind. Had he periled his political existence on the issue, no rational man can doubt that an amount of guilt, of misery, of disgrace, and of loss, would have been spared to England [and] to the civilized world, such as no other man had it in his power to arrest.[9]

In the end, however, it is probably the testimony of the leaders of the abolition movement that carries the most weight. The movement's heart and soul, Thomas Clarkson, praises Pitt's political efforts in his *History of the Abolition of the Slave Trade*, and most notably, through

William Pitt

all his political life William Wilberforce remained Pitt's close friend. For Pitt, a man who had few intimates, this is surely significant. As ever, Mr. Wilberforce gets the last word:

Mr. Pitt had foibles and, of course, they were not diminished by so long a continuance in office; but for a clear and comprehensive view of the most complicated subject in all its relations; for that fairness of mind which disposes a man to follow out, and when overtaken to recognize truth; for magnanimity, which made him ready to change his measures, when he thought the good of the country required it, though he knew he should be charged with inconsistency on account of the change; for the willingness to give a fair hearing to all that could be urged against his own opinions, and to listen to the suggestions of men, whose understanding he knew to be inferior to his own; for personal purity, disinterestedness, integrity, and love of his country, I have never known his equal.[10]

EDITOR'S NOTE:

This article is used by permission.

[1] Chatterton, E. Keble, *England's Greatest Statesman: A Life of William Pitt, 1759–1806* (Indianapolis, IN: Boss-Merrill, 1930).

[2] Ibid., p. 99.

[3] Ibid., p. 122.

[4] Ibid., p. 124, 150–153.

[5] Patrick Cleburne Lipscomb, *William Pitt and the Abolition of the Slave Trade*, dissertation, University of Texas, January 1960, p. 29.

[6] A.D. Harvey, *William Pitt the Younger: 1759–1806, A Bibliography* (Westport, CT: Meckler, 1989), p. 4.

[7] Robin Reilly, *William Pitt the Younger* (New York: Putnam's Sons, 1978), p. 255.

[8] Lipscomb, *William Pitt and the Abolition of the Slave Trade*, p. 5–6.

[9] Ibid., p. 14–15.

[10] Harvey, *William Pitt the Younger: 1759–1806, A Bibliography*.

Saturday, December 2, 1785: "Sir," wrote William Wilberforce in great distress, "I wish to have some serious conversation with you." Though Wilberforce possibly had not seen him for 14 years, John Newton, the writer of "Amazing Grace," was the one person whom he felt he could trust for spiritual advice. Whatever was said between them, it would unquestionably be held in complete confidence.

Wilberforce was just eight when his father died. In a few years his mother was struggling and sent her young son to London to live with his aunt Hannah and uncle William Wilberforce. By then, Hannah's brother John Thornton happened to be sponsoring John Newton's ministry. Although Newton lived in Olney, he would visit Thornton and Hannah Wilberforce when he came to London, and Hannah and "Uncle William" would return the visit. Mindful of the wasted years of his own youth, Newton had a passionate concern for young people. It wasn't long before "Master William" got to know the clergyman and looked up to him as a father figure.

Alarmed at her son's increasing circle of "Methodist" (evangelical) friends, Wilberforce's mother whisked him off back home to Hull. To her dismay, the head teacher of the grammar school there became converted, so she whisked him off again, this time to the grammar school in Pocklington,

John Newton

North Yorkshire, in the hope that he would lose all traces of these ghastly influences.

Hannah was terribly upset, but Newton wrote to remind her that though her nephew was exiled to a spiritually barren land, "The Lord can open springs and fountains in the wilderness. The word of grace and the throne of grace afford wells of salvation, from which he cannot be debarred." It was Newton's prayer that "like a tree of the Lord's planting," Master Wilberforce would "strike root downwards, and bear fruit upwards, and experience that the Lord is able to keep, establish, and comfort him."

Newton had been in Olney for 16 years, in an increasingly far-reaching ministry of preaching, pastoral care, correspondence, hymn writing, and publishing, when John Thornton procured him the living of St. Mary Woolnoth in Lombard Street, London. The church was in the heart of the capital city, close to the Bank of England.

The very year that the Newtons moved into their new home in London, Master Wilberforce had not only come of age but had become the newly elected MP for Hull, taking his seat in Parliament for the first time on October 31, 1780.

William Wilberforce enjoyed his new life, clubbing and socializing with his friends, among whom was his old

JOHN NEWTON: MENTOR TO WILLIAM WILBERFORCE BY MARYLYNN ROUSE college mate William Pitt. But five years later the young MP fell into a deep state of inner turmoil. A chance holiday with a friend, whom he discovered was a Christian, led him to take the Bible more seriously.

"Nothing convinces me of the dreadful state of my own mind," he confided in his journal, "as the possibility . . . of my being ashamed of Christ."

He suffered anguish as he tried to work out what to do. "I thought seriously this evening of going to converse with Mr. Newton," was his diary entry for November 30. Two days later, "Resolved again about Mr. Newton. It may do good; he will pray for me." He "kept debating in that unsettled way . . . whether to go to London or not" and eventually took the stage coach into the city and "inquired for old Newton; but found he lived too far off for me to see him."

In desperation, Wilberforce sat down and penned a note: "To the Rev. John Newton. Sir, I wish to have some serious conversation with you." The note ended, "PS. Remember that I must be secret, and that the gallery of the House [of Commons] is now so universally attended, that the face of a member of parliament is pretty well known."

The following day was Sunday. Again, he "had a good deal of debate" with himself about seeing Newton. Finally, despite "ten thousand doubts," he made his way to St. Mary Woolnoth for the evening service, and personally delivered his note afterward in the vestry. Newton was overwhelmed by what he could see in the making.

A date was arranged for their secret meeting. It was to be on Wednesday, at the Newtons' home in Charles Square, Hoxton. Wilberforce was highly apprehensive — it was a point of no return. "After walking about the Square once or twice before I could persuade myself, I called upon old Newton — was much affected in conversing with him — something very pleasing and unaffected in him."

To his amazement, he learned that his confidant "had always hopes and confidence that God would sometime bring me to Him." Wilberforce had been concerned that a Christian commitment would mean that he should resign and enter the church. But Newton

encouraged him instead to remain in politics, not to forsake his present friends, and not to rush into new acquaintances. He spoke gently of the workings of the Spirit of God in the heart of man and gave him a copy of his own "great turning day" experience to read, his *Authentic Narrative*.

"When I came away," wrote Wilberforce, "I found my mind in a calm, tranquil state, more humbled, and looking more devoutly up to God." Nevertheless, he swore Newton to secrecy.

The following Sunday, Wilberforce headed down to St. Mary Woolnoth with a lighter heart. He heard Newton preaching on the addiction of the soul to God. "Excellent. He shows his whole heart is engaged."

Wilberforce attended Newton's church every Sunday that month and was sometimes at his midweek lectures on Wednesdays. By Tuesday, December 20, he felt able to say, "He has my leave to mention my case to my aunt and Mr. Thornton." Newton wrote back a few days later, "I saw Mrs. Wilberforce [Aunt Hannah] today, and left her in tears of joy. She says you may depend on her strictly observing your requisitions."

Newton advised Wilberforce to attend the lectures of Thomas Scott at the Lock Hospital Chapel in London. Scott had himself been converted through Newton's patient and prayerful friendship, and was fast being regarded as the finest Bible commentator in the land. When Newton's friend Henry Venn came to hear of the changes in Wilberforce, he wrote excitedly to a colleague, "Mr. Wilberforce has been at the Chapel, and attends the preaching constantly. Much he has to give up! And what will be the issue, who can say?"

One Sunday, Wilberforce brought Newton home to Wimbledon with him to stay overnight, giving them more time to talk. The following evening they were seen walking together on the common. "Expect to hear myself now universally given out to be a Methodist," Wilberforce noted in his diary. Contrary to his former fears of such an association becoming publicly known, he added, "May God grant it may be said with truth."

With both men leading busy lives, correspondence became a practical solution.[1]

Conscious of the changes that Wilberforce's Christian commitment would require to his lifestyle, Newton reminded him of the honor and obligations to which he was called. "I believe you are the Lord's servant," he told Wilberforce, "and are in the post which he has assigned you; and though it appears to me more arduous, and requiring more self-denial than my own, I know that He who called you to it, can afford you strength according to your day, and I trust He will, for He is faithful to his promise."

For his encouragement, Newton directed Wilberforce to the examples of men in Scripture who had held responsible positions in government. "My heart is with you, my dear sir. I see, though from a distance, the importance and difficulties of your situation. May the wisdom that influenced Joseph and Moses and Daniel rest upon you. Not only to guide and animate you in the line of political duty — but especially to keep you in the habit of dependence upon God, and communion with him, in the midst of all the changes and bustle around you."

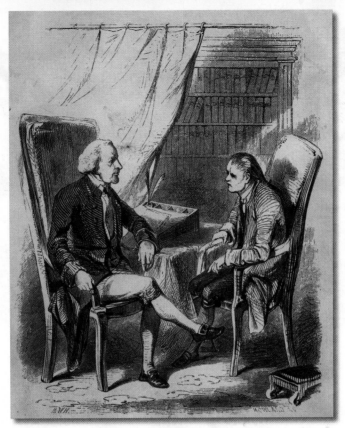

Wilberforce's interview with Newton

He gently steered Wilberforce into supporting Christian causes. "By this time," he wrote, "I know you too well to fear you will think me impertinent, if I occasionally submit to you such a case as I think may have a reference to the spread of the Good Gospel, and to promote the welfare of precious souls." Together they helped the shoemaker missionary William Carey get to India and the clergyman Richard Johnson join the First Fleet of convicts to Australia as their chaplain.

"Who can tell what important consequences may depend upon Mr. Johnson's going to New Holland! [Australia]" Newton exclaimed. "This small beginning may be like the dawn which advances to a bright day, and lead on to the happy time when many nations which now sit in darkness and in the region of the shadow of death, shall rejoice in the light of the Sun of Righteousness."

Wilberforce's resolution to take on the abolition of the slave trade appears in his journal for Sunday, October 28, 1787: "God Almighty has placed before me two great objects: the suppression of the Slave Trade and the Reformation of Manners."

On the day that Wilberforce wrote this, John Newton, his mentor, was with him. Wilberforce was concerned to know how he could carry with him the support of many who did not share his beliefs, without compromising his own, or as Newton summarized it, "How far we may accommodate ourselves to the prejudices of those about

Amazing Grace¹ by John Newton

Amazing Grace! How sweet the sound
That saved a wretch like me!
I once was lost, but now am found,
Was blind, but now I see.

'Twas grace that taught my heart to fear,
And grace my fears relieved;
How precious did that grace appear,
The hour I first believed!

Through many dangers, toils and snares,
I have already come;
'Tis grace has brought me safe thus far,
And grace will lead me home.

The Lord has promised good to me.
His Word my hope secures;
He will my shield and portion be,
As long as life endures.

Yea, when this flesh and heart shall fail,
And mortal life shall cease;
I shall possess, within the veil,
A life of joy and peace.

The earth shall soon dissolve like snow,
The sun forbear to shine;
But God, who called me here below,
Shall be forever mine.

(Last verse added in America at a later date)
When we've been there ten thousand years,
Bright shining as the sun,
We've no less days to sing God's praise
Than when we'd first begun.

us, with a hope of winning upon them, or at least of availing ourselves of their influence, to assist us in promoting those good designs which we cannot so well do without them." It was a question, Newton acknowledged, which "is indeed of great importance."

The advice he gave him, after much consideration, is as valid today as it was then. There were four areas of life it would be vital to keep in check.

1. His words, his example, and his conduct should say with Joshua, "As for me and my house, we will serve the Lord." He shouldn't be afraid or ashamed to be known to worship God, both privately and with his family. As far as his example, persuasion, and authority could influence them, he should try to see that everyone in his household avoided evil and was taught and encouraged to serve the Lord with him.

2. He should approve of and encourage the preaching of the gospel (regarded as foolish by the "wise" men of this world). He should worship regularly, at least on the Lord's Day, in a Gospel-centered fellowship. And at other times, as leisure and occasions offered, he would be as free as others to spend his time as he chose. This would demonstrate his preference for Christian company.

3. Though it wasn't wrong to occasionally be present in public worship where the gospel he loved wasn't preached, he should be cautious of making too many concessions of this sort, in case his presence and example might mislead others to think that doctrinal differences weren't as important as Scripture says they are. His preference for worshiping where the truth was preached,

backed up by his good character, might influence some of his colleagues to join him in the church he attended. Even though they might at first only come out of curiosity, they might, by the blessing of God, come to know the truth themselves.

4. As to complying with them in their amusements, it would be best to make short work of it and to say "No" in a firm tone to them all. When he had done this a few times, and was found to be inflexible, he would soon be freed from further demands. And he would still have "a thousand opportunities of showing them that his religion has not made him austere, unsociable, or scrupulous [fussy] in the affairs of common life."

Newton then set about making his own public contribution of information needed for the abolition debate by writing *Thoughts upon the African Slave Trade*. In this, he described what he had been involved in and witnessed as a slave trader, affirming his abhorrence for the slave trade, "a business at which my heart now shudders." The committee which later became the Anti-Slavery Society asked his permission to print 3,000 copies. They gave one to every Member of Parliament. Newton sent a copy to his old friend William Cowper, then one of Britain's foremost poets, who thought it likely to be "to all prudent persons, the most satisfactory publication on the subject."

Wilberforce became a target of slander and accusations. Newton tried to counteract this discouragement, reminding him of all that he had achieved so far on behalf of slaves, and pointing out how much his work would be valued in the future. To add some perspective to Wilberforce's personal trials, Newton wrote, "If you therefore meet with some unkind reflections and misrepresentations, from men of unfeeling and mercenary spirits, you will bear it patiently, when you think of Him who endured the contradiction of sinners against Himself."

"O my dear Sir," pleaded Wilberforce, "let not your hands cease to be lifted up, lest Amalek prevail."

When Newton knew that Wilberforce was presenting a motion in Parliament on the abolition of the slave trade he preached against the trade from his pulpit. Lombard Street was lined with city banks. With commercial interest being the chief obstacle to abolition, St. Mary Woolnoth, Lombard Street, was in a key location for the former slave trader to influence the hearts and consciences of the nation's bankers.

The impact that the Christians living around Clapham Common were having on affairs made a deep impression on Newton, who could see history in the making. "But when I think of you, Mr. Thornton, and a few of your friends," he wrote to Wilberforce, "I am ready to address you in the words of Mordecai — Who knoweth but God has raised you up for such a time as this!" Today there is a plaque at Wilberforce's local church, Holy Trinity, Clapham, which is inscribed in thanksgiving for the contribution to society made by Wilberforce, Thornton, and a few of his friends.

In the spring of 1795, Wilberforce was further disappointed in the House regarding the slave trade, and upset with himself for having been less prepared than on other occasions. Newton sought to comfort him. "You have acted nobly, Sir, in behalf of the poor Africans. I trust you will not lose your reward. But I believe the business is now transferred to a higher hand. If men will not redress their accumulated injuries, I believe the Lord will. I shall not wonder, if the Negative lately put upon your Motion, should prove a prelude to the loss of all our West India Islands. Nor dare I say, I shall be sorry, if there is no other way to procure the abolition of that inhuman traffic."

He assured him of many proofs that he had not labored in vain. "Though you have not fully succeeded in your persevering endeavors to abolish the slave trade as yet, the business is still in train, and since you took it in hand, the condition of the slaves already in our Islands has been undoubtedly meliorated."

Newton interpreted the nation's recent naval calamity as evidence of God's judgment against the oppressors. "Our boasted fleet was to sweep the seas, to cover the West Indies, and to do I know not what. But the Lord said, It shall not be. He blew with his wind, they were scattered, disconcerted, and driven back with heavy loss." As an experienced mariner, Newton realized how rare it was for such a long series of southwest storms to hit. "It is not Britannia, as our boasting song pretends, but the Lord who rules the waves, and them who sail upon them."

He admired the government in Britain, "Only in one point it fails — I fear it is merely political. It acknowledges not the Government of the Great God."

In 1791, New Jersey College, now Princeton University, awarded seven honorary doctorates. One was to John Newton, another to Thomas Jefferson, later to become the president of the United States.

Newton was the only former slave trader willing to give evidence before the Privy Council. His evidence was particularly weighty in support of abolition. Wilberforce asked his personal friend William Pitt, the prime minister, to come out of the House of Commons and personally escort Newton to introduce him to the Privy Council. Newton was examined on the 12th and 21st of May 1790. The minutes were published in parliamentary reports and in *An Abstract of the Evidence Delivered Before a Select Committee of the House of Commons in the Years 1790 and 1791 on the Part of the Petitioners for the Abolition of the Slave Trade.*

Newton wrote on one of the pages in his own copy of the Abstract, "I make no apology for speaking publicly against this trade. I dare not. Should I be silent; my conscience would speak loudly, knowing what I know. Nor could I expect a blessing on my ministry — though I should speak of the sufferings of Jesus, till I was hoarse."

Wilberforce sent Newton a copy of his book *Practical View*, hot off the press, thankful "to have published what I may term my manifesto — to have plainly told my worldly acquaintances what I think of their system and conduct and where it must end." He felt "a solid comfort from having openly declared myself as it were on the side of Christ," and having shown where his hopes for his country lay.

Newton was delighted. Again he drew an analogy with Daniel, "The power of the Lord in your favor, seems to be little less than

remarkable than in the three young men who lived unhurt and unsinged in the midst of the fire, or of Daniel who sat in peace in the den when surrounded by lions. It plainly shows that His grace is all-sufficient to keep us in any situation which his providence appoints us."

To Charles Grant, Newton declared, "What a phenomenon has Mr. Wilberforce sent abroad! Such a book, by such a man, and at such a time!"

When Wilberforce's renewed motion on abolition was carried by 124:49 in its first reading on May 30, 1804, his aging mentor and prayer supporter raced off a note in exuberance. "Though I can scarcely see the paper before me," the elderly Newton scrawled, "I must attempt to express my thankfulness to the Lord, and to offer my congratulations to you for the success which He has so far been pleased to give to your unwearied endeavors for the abolition of the slave trade, which I have considered as a millstone, sufficient, of itself sufficient, to sink such an enlightened and highly favored nation as ours to the bottom of the sea."

"Whether I who am within two months of entering my eightieth year shall live to see the accomplishment of the work, is only known to Him, in whose hands are all our times and ways, but the hopeful prospect of its accomplishment will, I trust, give me daily satisfaction so long as my declining faculties are preserved."

Newton lived to see the Act on the Abolition of the Slave Trade passed. He died on December 21, 1807. Wilberforce fought on for more than two decades. When he died in 1833, he had just lived long enough to be assured of the second Act — the Abolition of Slavery. It seems a seal on their friendship and their labors that these two godly men died at such marks in history — the one in the year of the abolition of slave trade and the other in the year of the abolition of slavery.

EDITOR'S NOTE:
Marylynn Rouse, Director of The John Newton Project. © The John Newton Project 2006. This article is reprinted by permission.

[1] Transcribed from John Newton's sermon notebook, Lambeth Palace Library, MS 2940 © Marylynn Rouse 2000 www.johnnewton.org

Charles James Fox was the third son of Henry Fox, Lord Holland, and his wife, Lady Georgina Caroline Fox. His mother was the eldest daughter of the son of Charles II, the second Duke of Richmond, and his wife, Sarah Cadogan. Fox's maternal grandmother, Sarah, was given in marriage to his grandfather Charles to settle a gaming debt between their respective fathers. The doomed couple was said to have loathed one another at first sight. They were both greatly relieved when their families parted them soon after the wedding: Sarah was sent off to school, and Charles sailed away on a grand tour of the continent.

Three years later when Charles returned from his travels, he went off to the opera on his first night back to postpone the inevitable — going home to his loathsome wife. There, in the box opposite him, sat the most beautiful creature he had ever seen. Instantly, Fox fell hopelessly in love with the charming young woman. Upon his inquiry as to her identity, he was utterly delighted to learn that the mystery woman was none other than the bride he had once despised!

This time, the elder Charles Fox wooed the young woman properly, and Sarah Cadogan fell passionately in love with him, too. Renowned for their great love affair, they were said to have kissed, cooed, and cuddled constantly. Their passionate marriage produced 12 children.

Elected to Parliament at age 19, Fox was initially more famous for his sense of style than his politics at the time. Following a European tour at age 19, he brought back to England the extravagant French court fashions of the Marconis,

Charles Fox

as well as male cosmetics. Although he was known as a great cricketer and walker, hundreds of cartoons attest to the fact he was overweight from his indulgences in food and drink, but he was also described as a dandy, famous for his sense of style. Decked out in frilly lace and brocade, he pranced around in shoes with red heels with his face caked in make-up and often wore a feather in his hat in the House of Commons. Despite Fox's outrageous image, his unattractiveness, clumsiness, and his sordid reputation, he was loved and respected by his friends and colleagues for his joviality, charm, and ebullience.

Fox made costly political mistakes, and his worst was when he formed a coalition with Frederick North in 1783, King George III's docile prime minister and front man during the American Revolution. Fox had long denounced North in the harshest of terms, but joined forces within because the alternative at the time was a coalition with a man that Fox opposed even more. Unfortunately for Fox, this move thoroughly undermined his credibility.

The king launched an all-out attack in 1784 on Fox's Westminster reelection. Realizing he could easily lose his reelection to Parliament, Fox made history as he brilliantly recruited his friend, the Duchess of Devonshire along with her sister and her friends, to assist him in getting votes. This was the first time in recorded history that women participated in a campaign.

Nathaniel Wraxall, in his book *Posthumous Memoirs*, recalled the Fox campaign. "These ladies, being previously furnished with lists of outlying voters, drove to their respective dwellings. Neither entreaties nor promises were spared." The Duchess and her friends got the voters to the polls, and as

CHARLES JAMES FOX: CHAMPION OF LIBERTY BY SUSAN WALES

caricatures and cartoons of the day show, she even shamelessly traded kisses for votes.

The opposition followed suit, enlisting the help of females including the Countess of Salisbury, but they were unsuccessful. It was the Duchess of Devonshire's renowned easy-going nature, and her "common touch" that made her enormously popular with the voters. Employing a number of other tactics, she literally bought votes by entering shops and often paying ten times the price for goods. The tactics worked, and Fox was reelected.

Throughout his political career, Fox championed the cause of freedom. His pursuits are best described by journalist Martin Kettle, "For the most part, though, his career reads like a roll of honour. Faced with a succession of the largest issues of the pre-democratic age, Fox repeatedly took his stand on what would now be called the liberal side."

In his personal life, Fox had fallen in love with a tall, elegant woman two years younger than he who called herself "Mrs. Armistead," although there was doubt a Mr. Armistead had ever existed. The alluring lady had liaisons with other high-ranking officials including the duke, who later became the Prince of Wales. During the early 1770s, Fox settled down blissfully with Elizabeth at her 30-acre spread in St. Anne's Hill, just south of the Thames River in Surrey. They were often seen laughing as they shopped for crockery together. Eventually, they were secretly married on September 28, 1795.

In 1806, Fox emerged from his retreat on St. Anne's Hill to make his last great parliamentary effort in the House of Commons on June 10, where he moved a resolution to abolish the slave trade on behalf of William Wilberforce's long years of efforts, "That this House, concerning the African Slave Trade to be contrary to the principles of justice, humanity, and sound policy, will, with all practical expedition, proceed to take effectual steps for abolishing the said trade, in such a manner and at such period, as may be deemed advisable."

Fox's next step was to introduce an abolition bill, but his health deteriorated during the summer of 1806, and it was not to be. His arms and legs swelled up, and he suffered chronic exhaustion. His doctors did a couple of painful "taps," in an effort to drain the excess fluids. For days, at St. Anne's Hill, he lay listlessly in a lounge chair as his wife read aloud from Virgil, John Dryden, Jonathan Swift, and other of his favorite authors. He was so loved that a large group of well-wishers gathered outside his home, in the street, to await the latest news.

On the afternoon of September 13, 1806, he managed to utter a few puzzling words to Elizabeth, "It don't signify, my dearest, dearest Liz." Next he declared, "I die happy," and he did. He was buried October 10 next to William Pitt in Westminster Abbey.

Upon learning of his death, his friend and colleague Sir Samuel Romilly wrote, "How unfortunate, that so soon after the country had recovered from its delusion respecting him, and was availing itself of his great talents, those talents should be extinguished."[1]

Sir Romilly described the mood at his funeral on October 10, 1806: "Most of the persons present seemed as if they had lost a most intimate and a most affectionate friend."[2]

In the early winter of 1807, Lord Grenville introduced Fox's motion for the Slave Traffic Bill into the House of Lords, where it passed by a large majority, notwithstanding the continued opposition of certain Peers, including Lord Eldon. Sent to the House of Commons, the Bill came up for the Committee stage on February 23, 1807, and was introduced rather lamely by Lord Howick. Following Sir Samuel Romilly's inspiring speech about Wilberforce's efforts to get this bill passed, members of Parliament voted overwhelmingly to support the bill that was passed at last, and on March 25, 1807, the measure reached the Statute Book.[3]

[1] *Memoirs of Sir Samuel Romilly*, Vol. II, p. 170.
[2] Ibid.
[3] 47 Geo. III, C.36 The Slave Trade Abolition Act, 1907.

England's future king, William, the Duke of Clarence in the House of Lords, was the abolition movement's most ardent opponent in the 1790s. The duke branded Wilberforce, Pitt, Burke, Fox, Sheridan, Canning, and other members of the movement, as "frauds or hypocrites!"

Born in Buckingham Palace in 1765, William was the third son of King George III and his wife, Queen Charlotte. At age 13 he joined the Royal Navy, where he served for 50 years. Eleven of those years were spent in active service in both war and peacetime under Captain Horatio Nelson in America and the West Indies.[1] Wined and dined enthusiastically by the plantation owners, Prince William's time spent in the West Indies was said to have deeply influenced his strong support of the slave trade.[2]

An early victory defending Gibraltar from recapture by the Spanish turned Prince William into somewhat of a celebrity when he returned to England. He was welcomed home by crowds of admiring young women and ballads and poems were written in his honor, but his ensuing lifestyle of gambling, drinking, and numerous love affairs deeply angered his father, the king. Prince William threatened his father to become a Member of Parliament if his father did not bestow him with the title of duke, so finally in 1797, the king appointed him the Duke of Clarence as the Keeper of Bushy Park.[3]

William, Duke of Clarence

Despite their differences, Prince William and his father, King George III, were united on the issues of the slave trade. Prime Minister Pitt the Younger said his inability to make the end of the slave trade a government issue could be explained by King George III's hatred of the abolitionists — equally as strong as the opposition of his son, the future king, William IV.[4]

"In his maiden speech before fellow members of the House of Lords, the Duke of Clarence called himself 'an attentive observer of the state of the negroes,' who found them well cared for and 'in a state of humble happiness.' On another occasion, he warned that Britain's abolishing the trade would mean the slaves would be transported by foreigners, 'who would not use them with such tenderness and care.'"[5]

Although the Duke of Clarence adamantly opposed abolishing the slave trade, when the bill was finally passed in 1807 he stood and applauded following Sir Samuel Romilly's tribute to William Wilberforce. In the film *Amazing Grace*, the duke snips to a colleague the Latin phrase, *noblise oblige* — meaning "I'm obliged to recognize an extraordinary commoner."

Prince William had never expected to become king but it became apparent he would at the death of

WILLIAM, DUKE OF CLARENCE

WILLIAM, DUKE OF CLARENCE: FOE OF ABOLITION BY SUSAN WALES

Princess Charlotte, the only heir of his brother, King George IV, who died in 1818. In 1830 when King George IV died, the Duke of Clarence, at the age of 65, became king, much to the consternation of the abolitionists. Ironically, the abolition of slavery was the one of the great accomplishments of his reign. The other great accomplishment was the reform bill that the king did not support but fearing a revolution, he passed.

[1] Many of the facts of this article were compiled from: "William IV." (1911). *Encyclopædia Britannica*, 11th ed. (London: Cambridge University Press, 1911).

[2] *The Encyclopedia of the Jamaican Heritage* Kingston, Twin Guinep Publishers, Sherlock, P. and Bennett, H. (1998).

[3] Royal Government, United Kingdom, *Royal Insight Magazine*, "Focus, Kings on the Sea," p. 4277, London, England.

[4] Adam Hotschild, "Against All Odds," *Mother Jones*, January–February 2004.

[5] Royal Government, "Focus, Kings on the Sea," p. 4277.

From the Family Prayers of William Wilberforce

Of all things, guard against neglecting God in the secret place of prayer.
— WILLIAM WILBERFORCE

We pray to Thee for all the dark corners of the earth,
For all who are suffering under the evils of slavery,
Or from injustice or cruelty of any kind.

Almighty God, may we live above the world,
Its low concerns and unsatisfying vanities,
And may we be still endeavouring to please Thee,
To root out every remainder of our natural corruption,
And to increase in every Christian grace.
May we indeed bear about us the likeness of our Heavenly Father,
And be doing good in our generation according to the will of God,
Until at length thou shalt receive us to Thyself,
and make us partakers of those pleasures which are at
Thy right hand for evermore.
— Amen

In the refreshing solitude of the English countryside, Thomas Clarkson's destiny was sealed. The night before, he had dined with friends at the home of Sir Charles and Lady Middleton, supporters of the abolitionist cause, whose conversation had so inspired him that he had pledged on the spot to join the struggle. Now, in the tranquility of his beloved outdoors, Clarkson weighed with a heavy heart, the gravity of his vow. Already ordained in the Anglican church, he had been sure of his ambition to become a minister, but now a daunting and urgent new calling seemed to beckon.

From that moment forward, Thomas Clarkson made the eradication of human slavery his life's work. As if singularly called and divinely appointed, of all the reformers and leaders of the abolitionist movement in Britain, Clarkson was the only one to make the cause his sole vocation.[1] Except for an eight-year period in the 1790s, when almost all work of the abolitionist movement in Britain ceased, the defeat of the slave trade and finally of slavery itself was his singular focus until his death in 1846, at age 84. He was, as his friend, the great English poet Samuel Taylor Coleridge affectionately dubbed him, "the Giant with one idea."[2]

By the time Thomas Clarkson was born in Wisbech in 1760, Europe had been transporting and selling slaves from the coast of West Africa for over 300 years.[3] Indeed, in the single century leading up to his birth, nearly two million slaves were transported by British vessels from Africa to the British West Indies.[4] Although Lord Mansfield had ruled

Thomas Clarkson

in 1772 that owning slaves had never "been in use or acknowledged by the law of England" and that the "claim of slavery [could] never be supported," the protection afforded by this precedent extended neither to the slave trade, nor to the colonies.[5] Furthermore, though trading in slaves was risky and often dangerous work, it could be especially lucrative. While reports of large profits were widely circulated, less well known were the slave trade's unimaginable horrors.

One exception was the widely publicized case of the slave ship *Zong*, whose captain conceived a way to defraud the voyage's underwriter by throwing overboard 133 chained Africans. He reasoned they were worth more dead than at auction. When the court declared the matter a "civil dispute between an insurance firm and a client," and that the deaths of the Africans amounted to the deaths of horses, the *Zong* became a rallying point for many in the growing abolitionist movement.[6]

As a student at Cambridge, Clarkson's initial interest in the question was solely a matter of academic ambition. Having already won the B.A. competition, he intended to make a name for himself as the first to win both prizes. But as he delved into his research, he found, with increasing revulsion, a horror he had never imagined. Suddenly, the essay took on new significance.

I had expected pleasure from the invention of the arguments, from the arrangement of them, from the bringing together, from the thought in the interim that I was engaged in an innocent test for literary honour. But all my pleasures were damped by the facts which were now continually before me. It was but one gloomy subject from morning to night. . . . I sometimes never closed my eyelids for grief. It became not so much a trial for academical reputation, as for the production of a work which might be of use to injured Africa.[7]

Clarkson won the competition and published his essay in 1786, bringing him closer to the emerging center of the British abolitionist movement. Most likely, Clarkson met William Wilberforce the following year, and in May, Clarkson, Wilberforce, and others, including some leading Quakers, formed the Society for the Abolition of the African Slave Trade.[8] Always with the ultimate goal of abolishing the whole institution of slavery, they strategically targeted the slave trade first since they knew its supporters were limited mostly to those with interests in the West Indian colonies. With the dismantling of the slave trade, the erosion of slavery itself would eventually follow.[9]

Though Wilberforce is given much-deserved praise for his efforts in Parliament, it was Clarkson who traversed the country (covering 35,000 miles in seven years) almost entirely on horseback to supply the Society with witnesses, testimony, and evidence to buttress their case.[10] Such was the interconnectedness and interdependence of the committee, that Clarkson, alluding to St. Paul's description of the Church, likened the Society to the human body.

For what, for example, could I myself have done if I had not derived so much assistance from the committee? What could Mr. Wilberforce have done in Parliament, if I . . . had not collected that great body of evidence, to which there was such a constant appeal? And what could the committee have done without the parliamentary aid of Mr. Wilberforce?[11]

In his role as chief investigator, Clarkson put himself in danger many times in order to obtain an accurate record of the crimes of slave traders. In his 1854 biography, James Elmes describes Clarkson's first investigative journey to Bristol (one of many he would eventually make), which, along with Liverpool was the key port for British slave ships.

On the way to Bristol he became afflicted with feelings of the deepest melancholy, for which he could not account. He trembled for the first time at the magnitude of the task he had undertaken; which was no less than to destroy one of the great branches of wealth and prosperity of the important commercial city within whose walls he was about to be a resident.[12]

Nevertheless, Clarkson's courage, or perhaps simply his deep conviction in the justness of his duty, overcame his fear.

Despite his courage, the campaign to end the slave trade was arduous and costly. Though not a wealthy man, he consistently used his own resources to help bring to trial slave ship captains and others who were implicated in the testimony he gathered. But it was not just his finances that suffered. He was running out of steam and the tide of public support for abolition was turning.

Clarkson believed that "since Christ died for mankind, all men were fundamentally equal," and thus the rumors of liberté, fraternité, egalité blowing from France excited him tremendously. He even traveled to Paris to lobby the new French government to extend the benefits of liberty to French slaves.[13] But when the promises of a lighter burden for the oppressed degenerated into violent anarchy and the new French government turned its bloodthirsty gaze toward the British throne, Clarkson's early vocal support for the French Revolution cost him and the abolitionist movement dearly. In Britain, the madness of the Jacobins in France was linked to the idea of expanded freedoms and liberty, and hence, the cause of liberation for slaves suffered a substantial setback. Hoping to avert a similar revolt in Britain, William Pitt's administration clamped down harshly on political speech. For nearly a decade, the abolitionist movement in Britain fell silent.

Discouraged and nearly broke, Clarkson retreated to the Lakes District of northern England where he married Catherine Buck in 1797.[14] They built a cottage and had a son, and it was during this time that Clarkson formed lasting friendships with the poets William Wordsworth and Samuel Taylor Coleridge.

The abolitionist movement resurged in 1804 and Clarkson set out again on his tour of the country, gathering information and rallying support wherever he went. With the death of the prime minister, William Pitt, in 1806, and the ascension of a new administration, the bill to abolish the British slave trade finally passed on February 23, 1807.

> With respect to the end obtained by . . . the great measure of the abolition of the Slave-trade . . . I know not how to appreciate its importance. . . . Can we contemplate the magnitude of crimes . . . without acknowledging that a source of the most monstrous and extensive wickedness has been removed also? But here, indeed, it becomes us peculiarly to rejoice; for though nature shrinks from pain, and compassion is engendered in us when we see it become the portion of others, yet what is physical suffering compared with moral guilt? . . . The body, though under affliction, may retain its shape; and, if it even perish, what is the loss of it but of worthless dust? But when the moral springs of the mind are poisoned, we lose the most excellent part of the constitution of our nature, and the divine image is no longer perceptible in us. . . . By a decree of Providence, for which we cannot be too thankful, we are made mortal. Hence the torments of the oppressor are but temporary; whereas the immortal part of

us, when once corrupted, may carry its pollutions with it into another world.

Clarkson heeded the call in his time. Would that there were men and women who would recognize the need, count the cost, and heed the call in ours.

EDITOR'S NOTE:
This article is used by permission.

1   Ellen Gibson Wilson, *Thomas Clarkson: A Biography* (New York: St. Martin's Press, 1990).
2   Earl Leslie Griggs, *Thomas Clarkson, the Friend of Slaves* (Ann Arbor, MI: University of Michigan Press, 1938), p. 26.
3   Robin Reilly, *William Pitt the Younger* (New York: Putnam's Sons, 1978), p. 249.
4   Patrick Cleburne Lipscomb, *William Pitt and the Abolition of the Slave Trade* dissertation, University of Texas, January 1960.
5   Reilly, *William Pitt the Younger.*
6   Wilson, *Thomas Clarkson: A Biography*, p. 10.
7   Clarkson, *The History of the Rise, Progress, and Accomplishment of the Abolition of the African Slave-Trade by the British Parliament*, p. 185–186.
8   Wilson, *Thomas Clarkson: A Biography.* (New York: St. Martin's Press, 1990) p xiii.
9   Reilly, *William Pitt the Younger*, p. 250.
10 Wilson, *Thomas Clarkson: A Biography*, p. 29.
11 Ibid., p. 3.
12 Lawrence W. Reed, "The Inspiring Story of Thomas Clarkson: A Student's Essay that Changed the World," January 2005, Mackinac Center for Public Policy.
13 Wilson, *Thomas Clarkson: A Biography*, p. 55.
14 Ibid., p. 95.

Big Ben is part of the building where Parliament is held.

An Inspiring Look at the Influence of William Wilberforce on Lives and Ministries Today

Wilberforce was determined and spent his entire political life in the pursuit of the abolition of the slave trade. It would be 26 more years before end slavery itself in the British Empire. Wilberforce died three days after this, his life complete. The bicentennial of this seminal event will be observed in 2007.

forbearance of Heaven by delaying this tardy act of justice.

The people we influence for good constitute the real and lasting monuments of our lives. I learned this lesson 20 years ago when I was in England giving lectures.

One day I asked my host if he could arrange a visit to the neighborhood of Clapham. This was the home of the great abolitionist William Wilberforce and his allies in fighting the British slave trade. I wanted to see the houses in which the Clapham Sect (as the abolitionists were called) had lived, the church in which they had worshiped, and any monuments that had been erected to honor their incredible campaign.

An English friend drove my wife and me to Clapham, a neighborhood on the fringes of London swallowed up by urban sprawl. When we arrived at dusk, a mist settled over the dark, cramped streets. The road twisted and turned up a hill, and my host announced, "We're getting close to where the Clapham Sect lived."

All I could see were dreary, whitewashed row houses. "Where's the Thornton farmhouse?" I asked, alluding to one of the Clapham Sect's principal residences.

"Oh, I forgot to tell you," he said. "All those farms were leveled in the period of industrial expansion and turned into city homes."

That was disappointing, but not as disappointing as what followed. We drove down to the Anglican Church on the green in Clapham. The mist had turned into a drizzle, and it was now almost completely dark. When we knocked on the church door, the rector appeared and greeted us.

"I want to see where Wilberforce preached," I told him, "and any monuments you have to Wilberforce and his group. He's my great hero," I explained.

The rector, who had been told we were coming, said, "Of course, of course. Come right this way."

We walked into the church, over stone floors, past the worn wooden pews to a place behind the altar. The rector proudly pointed to a stained-glass window in the apse. "There it is," he said.

The church was rather dark, so I squinted to see what he was pointing at.

The rector could tell I was having trouble. "Don't you see? There, in the center. The profile of Wilberforce."

The famous man's portrait occupied a small square in the center of one stained-glass window not more than eight or ten inches wide. Below the stained-glass window was a shelf with some brochures and a sign over it saying, "Clapham Sect Information, 50 p."

I tried to hide my disappointment, thanking the rector and paying the few pence for a couple of the brochures, but I was crestfallen. Wilberforce had changed the course of Western civilization. Through sheer perseverance and holy determination, he had fought the most detestable villainy of his age. This great man had brought the slave trade to an end, and only one pane of stained glass existed as a memorial? I couldn't believe it.

We thanked the rector and left. Escorted by my friend, my wife and I walked across the village green to where we had parked our car. I asked to stop for a moment in the middle of the green to collect my thoughts. As I did, I had a powerful moment of insight. In my mind's eye, I saw a long line of slaves in tattered loincloths, walking across the green with their chains falling off. *Of course,* I thought to myself, *Of course — that's it. Wilberforce's legacy is not in monuments or churches or stained-glass windows. It's in lives set free. The*

LIVING MONUMENTS BY CHUCK COLSON

stronger than God? Oh, be not weary of well-doing. Go on in the name of God, and in the power of His might. . . ."

I saw Wilberforce as the perfect illustration of how a Christian should behave in the political arena. He gave his first allegiance to God and to His kingdom over his allegiance to the Tory Party. In fact, Wilberforce lost his relationship for a while with his great friend William Pitt, England's prime minister. He certainly lost his chance to become prime minister of England himself because of his fervent commitment to the cause of abolition, against which the power of the British Empire was standing foursquare. Wilberforce was threatening the Empire's biggest source of commerce.

The great abolitionist's decades-long battle began on the foggy Sunday morning of October 25, 1787. Wilberforce sat at his desk thinking about his conversion and his calling. Had God saved him only to rescue his own soul from hell? He could not accept that. If Christianity were true and meaningful, it must not only save, but also serve. It must bring God's compassion to the oppressed as well as oppose the oppressors.

Wilberforce dipped his pen in the inkwell and wrote in his diary, "Almighty God has set before me two great objectives, the abolition of the slave trade and the reformation of manners [morals]."

It was the great genius of Wilberforce that he realized that attempts at political reform were futile without at the same time changing the hearts and minds of the people. The abolitionists realized

black men and women who are no longer subject to slavery are the living monuments of William Wilberforce and his work. Generations of people can thank Wilberforce for changing their destinies.

I'd wanted to see a monument to Wilberforce because he had been the first serious inspiration and Christian role model for me. Soon after my conversion I learned about him and was struck by his deep spirituality, including his three hours of prayer each day and his deep fellowship with the Clapham sect, with whom he persevered over decades to rid England of the abominable slave trade. In fact, for many years I carried in my Bible the words out of a letter from Charles Wesley to Wilberforce: "Unless God has raised you up for this very thing, you will be worn out by the opposition of men and devils, but if God be for you who can be against you? Are all of them together

Nov 21st monday 1784. Began my journal with a view to make myself humble & watchful ___

Bacon says, Great Changes are easier than small ones ___

Sunday 1787   God Almighty has placed before me two great objects the Suppression of the Slave Trade & the Reformation of manners.

Sunday 1/2 oClock Feby 22d 1807   ... God never surely had more Cause for Gratitude than now as carrying the great object of my life to which a gracious Providence directed my thoughts 26 or 27 years ago ... my Endeavours in 1787 or 1788 ... let me praise thee to my whole heart.

One of Wilberforce's diary entries

it *A Practical View of the Prevailing Religious System of Professed Christians in the Higher and Middle Classes in this Country Contrasted with Real Christianity.*

The title itself was a scandal to the established religion, a direct challenge to the corrupted church of his day. But the book's impact can scarcely be overstated. It became an instant bestseller, and remained one for the next 50 years. Biographer Garth Lean quotes one observer who wrote: "[The book] was read at the same moment, by all the leading persons in the nation. An electric shock could not be felt more vividly and instantaneously."

A Practical View is credited with helping spark the second Great Awakening (the first was begun by Wesley) and its influence was felt throughout both Europe and America. With the outlawing of the slave trade in 1807 came an 18-year battle for the total emancipation of the slaves. Social reforms swept beyond abolition to clean up child labor laws, poorhouses, prisons, and to institute education and health care for the poor. Evangelism flourished, and later in the century, missionary movements sent Christians fanning across the globe.

that they could never succeed in eliminating slavery without addressing the greater problems of cultural malaise and decay.

But it was a difficult concept to explain. In the hope of reaching Pitt and other friends, Wilberforce wrote a book in 1797 and called

This was the great legacy of Wilberforce: One man, convicted by his conscience and his God that he had to oppose the slave trade, not only abolished a great social evil but also reformed the morals of England.

Two hundred years later, as I labored in the prisons, what was clear to Wilberforce became clear to me: We could not simply deal with a structural problem of society — be it slavery or crime — without also attempting to reverse a society's moral decline.

Like Wilberforce, I had a background in politics. I had my own "great change" in 1973, during the midst of the Watergate scandal, accepting Christ in a flood of tears in a friend's driveway. After serving a seven-month prison term for Watergate-related offences, I realized I had been sent to prison for a purpose.

Behind bars, I had encountered people who had no hope, no one to care what happened to them. Once released, some 65 percent of these inmates would commit more crimes and end up back behind bars. Tragically, the children of prisoners are more likely than any other group to follow their parents into the "family business": crime. Clearly, these men needed a champion — and I was determined to give them one. In 1976, Prison Fellowship was born in a converted townhouse five miles outside Washington in Arlington, Virginia.

Within a few years, I realized that we were evangelizing more and more prisoners every year — yet the prison population continued to rise. It was at that point that I learned of the work of William Wilberforce. It struck me that we couldn't just evangelize the prisons; like Wilberforce, we also had to change the culture. And the place to begin was the American family.

Much of our society's moral collapse centers on the disintegration of the family. Research overwhelmingly confirms that boys are far less likely commit crimes if they grow up in intact homes led by a married mother and father. A 2004 study by Cynthia Harper and Sara McLanahan found that boys reared in single-parent homes and stepfamilies are more than twice as likely to end up in prison, compared to boys reared in an intact family.

Girls reared in single-parent homes, homes broken by divorce, or homes that include cohabiting adults, are significantly more likely to suffer sexual abuse and early pregnancy than girls reared within an intact, married family.

Clearly, those who encourage couples to cohabit rather than marry, and to have children out of wedlock, are wreaking great damage on our culture.

Most academics in the 20th century believed that crime was a result of sociological factors. A generation of liberals in academia and government promoted the view that if only the evils of society — such as poverty, unemployment, and racism — were overcome, crime would disappear.

They were wrong. Psychologists Stanton Samenow and Samuel Yochelson, in their landmark 1977 study, *The Criminal Personality*, discovered that, with their subjects, crime was a *moral* problem. They concluded that criminals, not society, are the cause of crime. These findings found further support in Wilson and Hernstein's definitive 1986 study *Crime and Human Nature*. The two Harvard professors concurred that crime is essentially a function of lack of moral training during the morally formative years. In other words, crime is a moral problem that demands a moral solution.

I began to address our country's moral breakdown in the 1980s in speeches and in articles. Then, in 1984, I began writing a column in *Christianity Today*. Seven years later, in 1991, I began a daily radio program called *BreakPoint*, a commentary on news and trends from a biblical world view. The program now reaches millions of listeners and e-mail subscribers. The world view message was expanded into a book, *How Now Shall We Live?* (with Nancy Pearcey) in 1999.

A few years ago, Prison Fellowship created a new division called the Wilberforce Forum, intended to help Christians approach life with a biblical world view so that they can in turn shape culture from a biblical perspective. Using the talents of Christian thinkers and writers, we seek to help Christians think and live Christianly not only in church and family circles, but also in the public square.

We carried this goal a step further in 2004 when Prison Fellowship began an ambitious program to train ordinary Christians to identify, articulate, and live out a biblical world view — and then teach it to others. The Centurions program pulls together 100 Christians at a time, from all over America and from all walks of life, into a year-long distance learning program and ongoing web community. We cover everything from politics to education to the arts. Centurions are then taught how to design their own world view teaching strategy and teach others.

Our Centurions have the potential to accomplish the same thing Wilberforce did — to raise up an army of Christians equipped to call the Church to greater faithfulness to God and to change our culture one person at a time by defending biblical truth.

In the first decade of the 21st century, Christians are increasingly — and rightfully — taking their place in the political square, even though others would prefer that we stay quietly at home, reading our Bibles, and leave politics to them. Whenever they see us invading what they consider *their* turf, they get the epithets ready: "Bigot." "Zealot." "Extremist."

But have we really "come to a pretty pass when religion is allowed to invade public life" as Lord Melborne complained more than two hundred years ago in response to Wilberforce — and as secular critics complain today in response to us? Is Christian influence in politics today truly "a far greater threat to democracy than was posed by communism" as the *New York Times* once claimed? Nonsense.

"Wilberforce understood that while people may ignore the truth, they still recognize it when they see it. So he looked for ways to remind people of what they already knew in their hearts."[1]
– Chuck Colson

William Wilberforce is a special inspiration for today's "extremists" who stride into the public square and stay there, despite debasement, derision, and defeat, as long as we believe that's where God wants us.

As Wilberforce wrote in the conclusion to *A Practical View of Christianity:* "I must confess equally boldly that my own solid hopes for the well-being of my country depend, not so much on her navies and armies, nor on the wisdom of her rulers, nor on the spirit of her people, as on the persuasion that she still contains many who love and obey the gospel of Christ. I believe that their prayers may yet prevail."

The confidence of Wilberforce was not misplaced. May the same hope prevail for Christians today as we, like Wilberforce, cling to biblical truth, resist barbaric injustice, and strive to change the heart of a nation. May we, like the long-ago Clapham Sect, leave behind living monuments: The shackles of sin broken, and millions of lives transformed.

EDITOR'S NOTE:

Chuck Colson is a popular and widely known author, speaker, and radio commentator. A former presidential aide to Richard Nixon and founder of the international ministry Prison Fellowship, he has written several books — including Born Again, Loving God, How Now Shall We Live, *and* The Good Life — *that have shaped Christian thinking on a variety of subjects. His radio broadcast,* BreakPoint, *airs daily to five million listeners. In 1993, Colson was awarded the prestigious Templeton Prize for Progress in Religion; the one million dollar prize — along with all speaking fees and book royalties — are donated to Prison Fellowship. He and his wife, Patty, have three children and five grandchildren. This article is reprinted by permission.*

[1] Chuck Colson, "Staying Power: Wilberforce, Slavery — and Abortion," *Christian Examiner,* http://www.christian examiner.com/Articles/Chuck%20Colson/Art_Jan03_Colson.html (accessed Nov. 17, 2006).

SILENCE IS NOT GOLDEN

An Inspirational Look at How You, Too, Can Grow in Faith, Knowledge, and Understanding and Make a Difference in the World Today

At a time in world history when moral, physical, and spiritual depravity is rampant, it is refreshing to be reminded of the life and legacy of William Wilberforce, a champion for justice. He not only worked in the latter 1700s and early 1800s in his native England and her colonies against the injustices and inhumane atrocities perpetrated against slaves, but he also spent the rest of his life working for the abolition of this evil institution. What an inspiration — especially during this time of man's gross inhumanity to man displayed in attempted racial genocide, jihad, ethnic cleansing, and slavery — to know that people of faith, knowledge, and understanding in earlier years can motivate us to take up the mantle even today and become God's mouthpiece for justice!

Wilberforce's mission was to call his nation to repentance and transformation. His impact on slavery and the abolition of the slave trade offers hope to those who have become bone and spiritually weary in the fight for equal opportunity and justice for all. It is encouraging to the committed warriors who are overwhelmed by such pandemic diseases as AIDS that threaten entire generations of people, simply because they do not have the necessary resources they need (due to the pigmentation of their skin). The road was long and perilous, but Wilberforce persevered until his death. The road is long and perilous for us today; but with tenacity and faith in God, we must persevere as well!

Admittedly, during Wilberforce's tenure in the Parliament, England's culture was known for her moral "callousness, indifference, and hedonism. The empire's cultural elite had made great strides in normalizing debauchery, [depravity, sin, and wickedness]"

Restraining irons used on slaves

SILENCE IS NOT GOLDEN: WILBERFORCE AND HIS IMPACT TODAY BY JEFFREY AND LAKITA WRIGHT AND EVANGELINE CAREY (www.claphamfellowship.com). In fact, slavery and slave trading were at their peak. God used Wilberforce to address, cajole, and warn his own race about dehumanizing and marginalizing a people that God made in His own image and after His likeness. The poor and oppressed that God wanted delivered were millions of African slaves. Wilberforce used his time, talents, and resources for this purpose.

While the society around him continued to spiral downward, Wilberforce warned slave traders, masters, and oppressors that slavery was a cancer on the landscape of their society that must be radically excised. Pursuing his beliefs caused Wilberforce to be the Moses of his day.

Wilberforce was born August 24, 1759, in Hull, England. His life was distinguished by privilege, wealth, and position. Upon his conversion to Christianity, he took up the cause of the poor and oppressed slaves. He felt guilty and ashamed that, under their authority and watch, the whole Parliament of Great Britain had allowed the slave trade. This man of God used his inherited wealth and his position as a means to turn the tide.

Until his death in 1833, public opinion and the economic self-interest of his own nation were overwhelmingly against him. He also suffered many calamities, including threats to his life, the loss of friends, insurmountable political

First page from one of the bills to abolish slavery in England

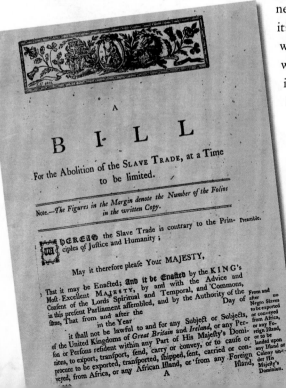

pressures, vicious slander, family issues, and severe health concerns. In spite of all this, Wilberforce persisted in the fight for justice. Still, it took him more than 20 years to persuade the House of Commons and the House of Lords to put abolition into law.

Wilberforce's life and legacy show that God still raises up spokespersons to warn the disobedient nations of impending doom — of God's wrath and judgment against those who oppress the poor and pervert justice. In this fallen world, the grievous injustices are wake-up calls for men and women of faith, character, and convictions to stand up and be counted. We can make a difference wherever the cancer of bigotry and intolerance ensnare a people. We can make a difference wherever the cancer of wickedness and oppression ensnare a people. We should remember that silence on the difficult moral and societal issues of our day — including poverty, inequality, and injustice — is not golden. Instead, it can be deadly. We must ask ourselves, "What is the slavery of today?" More importantly, we need to ask, "What could God be calling us to do about it?" Wilberforce serves as an inspiration as an individual who not only changed his nation but also changed the world. We must now be the voices that speak out against injustice, the hands that work for positive change, and the feet that march until "judgment run down as waters, and righteousness as a mighty stream" (Amos 5:24).

(Sources)

Life Application Study Bible (Wheaton, IL: Tyndale House Publishers, Inc., 1996).

Charles F. Pfeiffer, Howard F. Vos, and John Rea, editors, *Wycliffe Bible Dictionary* (Peabody, MA: Hendrickson Publishers, Inc., 1998).

http://www.brycchancarey.com/abolition/wilberforce.htm. Accessed: 8/25/06.

http://www.claphamfellowship.com. Accessed: 6/21/06.

http://www.rts.edu/quarterly/fall97/qa.html. Accessed: 8/25/06.

http://www.spartacus.schoolnet.co.uk/REwilberforce.htm. Accessed: 8/25/06.

EDITOR'S NOTE:
Dr. Hill describes how William Wilberforce and his friends and associates have influenced people of faith and values today.

William Wilberforce

The 200th anniversary of the abolition of the slave trade in 2007 brought the name of William Wilberforce, who lived from 1784 to 1812, to the forefront of public attention in Great Britain. People throughout the world will make pilgrimages from London traveling the same roads Wilberforce traveled from his birthplace of Hull in the county of Yorkshire, and the community of Clapham, the birthplace of his great call from God.

Wilberforce also spent time at Moggerhanger Park, which is only 60 miles north of London. In those days, the roads were dreadful — riddled with deep potholes that sometimes caused carriages to turn over. The Great North Road between London and York was no exception, but for Wilberforce a welcome respite awaited — an overnight stop at a family home, a day's journey from Wilberforce's home in Clapham, south of London.

The Thorntons

Two hundred years ago, Godfrey Thornton, a first cousin of Henry Thornton and his sister, who was the wife of Wilberforce's Uncle William, owned Moggerhanger Park. After Wilberforce's father died, he was sent to live with his Uncle William and his wife until his mother feared they and the Thorntons were turning young William into an evangelical Methodist. Evangelicalism was highly unpopular at the time due to its association with Methodism. The rich and powerful of the English Establishment derided

Henry Thornton

Methodism as religious "enthusiasm." Henry Thornton, a Member of Parliament for the London constituency of Southwark, was a leading member of the "Clapham" group of evangelicals. It was his home, Battersea Rise, on the north boundary of Clapham Common, where the Claphamites met.

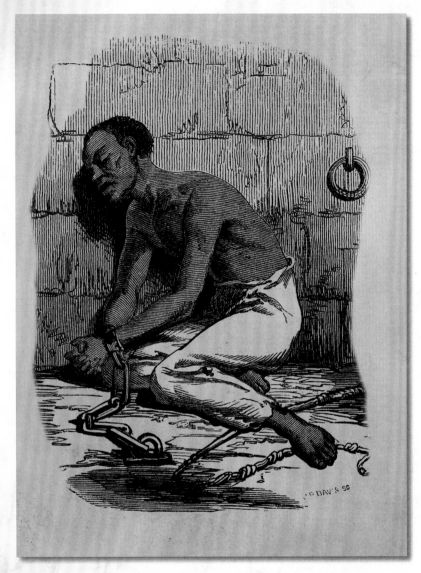

Illustration of a slave in chains

Henry Thornton was a generous philanthropist. He often visited the Moggerhanger area where the famous evangelist John Berridge, who often ministered with John Wesley, lived in a neighboring parish. Moggerhanger Park provided a convenient country retreat for prayer and vital discussion of the many far-reaching issues that the Clapham group was involved in. They are best remembered for their great achievement in the abolition of slavery throughout the British Empire, but their work also included striving for moral reform and the spiritual renewal of the nation.

Moggerhanger Park —Spiritual Heritage

In the 21st century, Moggerhanger Park has become the home of several evangelical ministries that follow in the tradition of Wilberforce and the Clapham group. Their work includes a range of projects from straightforward evangelism to practical community work — working with families to cut down the level of family breakdown, teenage pregnancy, drug addiction, and crime.

After many years of ministry in the poorest and most violent parts of London, the evangelical groups are grateful that Moggerhanger Park provides a quiet place for prayer and the development of their teaching ministry. Miraculously, the group of ministries knew nothing of the history of the house until after they acquired it. They simply moved there because they believed that it was God's will for them to do so.

The leading ministry at Moggerhanger Park is the "Centre for Contemporary Ministry," whose mission is to train and equip Christian leaders to communicate the gospel in the 21st century. Just as leaders of the area did in Wilberforce's day, the Centre continually monitors the spiritual health of the nation and alerts leaders to the significance of current issues where there

Heritage

Over 400 years old, the original house was Tudor, and then in 1792 it was enlarged and renovated by Sir John Soane, the most famous architect of the Georgian period. He also built many famous buildings and great houses in England, including the Bank of England in London and 10 Downing Street, the home of British prime ministers. The State Room on 10 Downing Street is an exact copy of one of the rooms in Moggerhanger Park, which Soane built first. Moggerhanger Park is Grade One listed as a national heritage site as it is the only one of Soane's country houses left in England capable of full restoration to its original design. The original plans and handwritten notes stored in the "Sir John Soane Museum" in London have been used in its restoration. Its beautiful architecture was revealed and people have begun coming from all over the world to see it. Since acquiring Moggerhanger Park, the evangelical groups have lovingly restored the 27-bedroom country mansion from its derelict condition.

Moggerhanger Park provided a convenient country retreat for prayer and vital discussion of the many far-reaching issues that the Clapham group was involved in.

Evangelism

Based in a house with such an outstanding heritage has given the ministries amazing opportunity for evangelism as visitors always ask two questions, "Who used to live here?" and "What are you doing with it now?" The answers to these questions provide an ideal opportunity for sharing the Christian faith.

Slavery, Past and Present

Members of the Centre have organized a national exhibition of slavery past and present in celebration of the 200th anniversary for the abolition of the slave trade. The square rigger "slave ship" used in the film *Amazing Grace* sailed from Cornwall with a Royal Navy escort to Liverpool and Bristol — the two main centers of the 18th century slave trade in England. It then sailed through the English Channel and up the River Thames to a mooring in central London where thousands of visitors saw it. The ship contains replicas of the cramped slave quarters on the lower deck, and also many of the cruel implements used by the slavers and information about the abolitionists and their Christian faith.

Following the exhibition in London, the exhibit will move to Moggerhanger Park where it will be used as a major national educational facility for schools and universities, as well as for the general public. By locating the exhibition at Moggerhanger, the ministry will lecture about the faith of the evangelical abolitionists led by Wilberforce and Thornton. The exhibition features aspects of modern slavery, including people trafficking in many parts of the world. This gives us the opportunity to demonstrate something of what is being done today by the Christian ministry that shares the same faith and convictions as those who lived here 200 years ago.

History is rich with testimonies of men and women whose transformed lives helped to change the course of history. Such is true of the life of abolitionist William Wilberforce. After the death of his father, young Wilberforce was raised by his mother, his aunt, and his uncle. He was exposed to the teachings of John Wesley and was won by the friendship and mentorship of former slave trader John Newton. Newton's rendition of the song "Amazing Grace" exposed the raw truth of the wretchedness of life without Christ and set Wilberforce on a path that would win him a place in the annals of history as one of the world's greatest abolitionists.

Revival and enlightenment go hand in hand. Once Wilberforce repented and personally accepted Christ into his life, he was ready to be used by God. In the annals of history, the noted statesman and freedom fighter stands in good company indeed.

Consider: Moses was a reluctant prophet; David was a murderer; Esther was hidden away in a harem; Rahab was a harlot, as was Mary Magdalene; Paul was a murderer of Christians, we all know the testimonies of the saints of old. History is consistent. God uses imperfect humanity to deliver His grace!

Ask Rosa Parks, the seamstress, and Martin, the dreamer. If they were here, they would tell as surely as William Wilberforce would that it is only God's amazing grace that can transform a stony heart into a heart of service. It is no wonder that William Wilberforce's name and contributions to the cause of emancipation are often coupled with other notable freedom fighters, such as Dr. Martin Luther King Jr.

Like many who have yet to be tried in the fire, young Wilberforce was judgmental as a student. Having led a sheltered life, he was shocked by the conduct of many of his fellow students, and even wrote: "I was introduced on the very first night of my arrival to as licentious a set of men as can well be conceived. They drank hard, and their conversation was even worse than their lives."

Although Wilberforce was initially shocked by the lifestyles of his peers, he eventually sampled a hedonistic lifestyle for a season, yet the prayers of his loved ones covered him, and he didn't stray for long.

After school, Wilberforce chose a career in politics, spending nearly ten thousand pounds to get elected as a member of Parliament. In the course of events, William became an evangelical, which led to his becoming interested in social reform; especially improving working conditions in factories.

While seated in Parliament, Wilberforce was approached by Lady Middleton (Albinia Townshend, elder sister of Thomas Townshend, 1st Viscount Sydney). She asked him to use his power in Parliament to help abolish the slave trade. Wilberforce wrote, "I feel the great importance of the subject and I think myself unequal to the task allotted to me," but he agreed to do his best. On May 12, 1789, Wilberforce made his first speech against the slave trade.

Wilberforce's spiritual journey had led him to become recognized as one of the leaders of the anti-slave trade movement. The Bible says to humble yourself in the sight of the Lord, and He will elevate you. This truth is apparent in the life of this historical servant.

Wilberforce and his associate, William Grenville, stood against opposition to their efforts. In a speech before his colleagues, Grenville said that trade was "contrary to the principles of justice, humanity, and sound policy." When the vote was re-cast, a huge majority in the House of Commons and the House of Lords backed the proposal, passing the law on March 25, 1807. Support for the campaign grew, and with friends including Beilby Porteus, the Bishop of London, Wilberforce continued to lobby for justice for slaves in the British Empire.

In the ensuing battle, stiff fines did not stop the slave trade. While some advocated immediate emancipation of the slaves, Wilberforce felt: "It would be wrong to emancipate (the slaves). To grant freedom to them immediately would be to insure not only their masters' ruin, but their own. They must (first) be trained and educated for freedom."

Prior to his retirement, Wilberforce joined the emancipation campaign. He died days after the 1833 Slavery Abolition Act was passed (an act granting liberty to all slaves in the British Empire).

During his lifetime, William Wilberforce championed many causes, emancipation being the most acknowledged. His other passions included missionary work to India, founding the Bishopric of Calcutta; animal protection efforts, founding the Royal Society for the Prevention of Cruelty to Animals; and what he called the "Reformation of Manners." It was at his suggestion, together with Bishop Porteus, that the Archbishop of Canterbury appealed to King George III to issue his "Proclamation for the Discouragement of Vice." Wilberforce also supported Christian Education.

Beilby Porteus

As a modern-day minister of the gospel of Jesus Christ, and a mother and Civil Rights Activist, I am inspired by the life of this great leader. My platform as a post-abortive, pro-life speaker, an advocate for family values and Christian/Bible based education and wholesome media, I recognize the impact of the contribution to our history. Finally, as the daughter, granddaughter, and niece of civil rights icons A.D. King, Daddy King, and Martin and Coretta King, I enjoy studying the life and philosophy of Wilberforce.

All can benefit from the example of the faith, courage, and conviction of William Wilberforce. He allowed himself to be groomed by God to be a champion for justice for all people. Wilberforce grew to become a devoted Christian, husband, father, and pillar of his community. His place as a hero in history is well deserved. Wilberforce University and the 17th-century house in which he was born, known today as Wilberforce House Museum in Kingston upon Hull, are testimonies to his life and contributions.

EDITOR'S NOTE:

Alveda C. King is a former member of the Georgia House of Representatives and the founder of King for America. King has an M.A. in business management from Central Michigan University. She received her Doctorate from Saint Anselm College. King is a prominent pro-life speaker and often speaks on college campuses about pro-life issues. She is the niece of civil rights leader Martin Luther King, Jr.

Timeline

1562   First English slaving expedition by Sir John Hawkins

1619   First recorded cargo of Africans landed in Virginia

1625   First English settlement on Barbados

1626   First boatload of African slaves to the island of St. Christopher in the British West Indies, known today as St. Kitts

1631   Charles I granted monopoly on Guinea trade to a group of London merchants

1655   British capture of Jamaica as part of Cromwell's "Grand Design"

1672   Royal Africa Company granted charter to carry Africans to the Americas

1772   Slavery declared illegal in England, Wales & Ireland (the Somerset case)

1778   Slavery declared illegal in Scotland

1781   Over 100 African slaves thrown overboard from the slave ship *Zong*

1783   Committee on the Slave Trade established by Quakers' Meeting for Sufferings

1787   Society for the Abolition of the Slave Trade founded: Granville Sharp as president of a mostly Quaker committee

1791   August 23 — St. Domingue (Haiti) slave revolt

1792   Resolution for gradual abolition of the slave trade defeated in House of Lords

1805   Bill for Abolition passed in Commons, rejected in House of Lords

1807   March 25 — Slave Trade Abolition Bill passed in the British Parliament

1808   US abolished the slave trade

1833   Abolition of Slavery British Empire Bill passed, with effect from 1834 and providing for up to six year "apprentice" transition. £20M voted as compensation to slave owners

1838   August 1 — enslaved men, women and children in British Empire became free

1842   Britain & United States signed Webster-Ashburton Treaty, banning slave trade on high seas

1848   Emancipation by the French of their slaves

1850   The Fugitive Slave Law passed in the United States

1865   Slavery finally abolished in United States territories

1888   Slavery abolished in Brazil

SLAVERY FACTS AND FIGURES COMPILED FOR SET ALL FREE,
THE BICENTENNIAL OF THE SLAVE ACT BY CHURCHES TOGETHER IN ENGLAND

Coin to
commemorate
the abolition of
slavery

AM I NOT A MAN & A BROTHER

West African native canoe full of captives to be sold as slaves

Facts and Figures on Africa

- Of the African slaves transported to the Americas, males outnumbered females by a ratio of 2:1.

- Most enslaved African males were between the ages of 15 and 35.

- Male children less than 15 years of age made up around 15 – 20 percent of the Africans transported to the Americas.

- Very few elderly Africans were transported across the Atlantic.

- Although it is estimated that between 9–12 million Africans were transported to the Americas, there are no accurate figures for the myriad number smuggled across the Atlantic to avoid tax, duty, and regulations.

- It has been estimated that over a million Africans died between the time they were captured and forced onto ships.

- Around 40 percent of African slaves were transported to Brazil.

- Around 40 percent were shipped to the Caribbean.

- The remainder were shipped to the United States and the Spanish speaking territories.

- Prior to using Africans, Europeans enslaved indigenous peoples in the Americas. On the larger Caribbean islands of Cuba, Hispanola, and Jamaica, Arawak and Carib "Indians" were enslaved by Europeans to work in mines and enclosures. However, overwork, disease and general brutality led to the rapid depletion of their population within several generations.

Facts and Figures on Europe

- European indentured labor (a fixed time of service) was also used in the United States and islands such as Barbados.

- Bristol, like Liverpool, became legally involved in the slave trade after the London-controlled Royal Africa Company lost its charter in 1698. It is estimated that between 1698 and 1807, nearly 2,100 slave-related ships set out from the port.

- The voyage from Britain to Africa could take anything from four weeks to over two months depending on the weather, size of the ship, and route taken.

- In the 18th century, slavers from Bristol ranged from 27 tons to 420 tons.

- The triangular trip could take a year to complete. Many of the ship's crew were paid in advance for the initial voyage to Africa. (Most used this money to pay off debts, buy provisions, or give to their families.)

- As well as Liverpool, London, and Bristol, other British slave trading ports included Lancaster, Whitehaven, Portsmouth, Plymouth, Glasgow, and Exeter.

[1] Set the Captives Free, Set All Free website. Used by permission of Churches Together in England http://www.cte.org.uk 27 Tavistock Square, London

A

B I L L

[AS AMENDED BY THE COMMITTEE]

To prevent the Importation of Slaves, by any of His Majesty's Subjects, into any Islands, Colonies, Plantations, or Territories, belonging to any Foreign Sovereign, State, or Power; and also, to render more effectual a certain Order, made by His Majesty in Council on the fifteenth day of August one thousand eight hundred and five, for prohibiting the Importation of Slaves (except in certain Cases) into any of the Settlements, Islands, Colonies, or Plantations, on the Continent of *America*, or in the *West Indies*, which have been surrendered to His Majesty's Arms during the present War.

Note.—*The Figures in the Margin denote the Number of the Folios in the written Copy.*

N. B. *The Clause marked (A.) was added by the Committee.*

WHEREAS it is expedient to prevent the supplying the Islands, Colonies, and Territories, belonging to any Foreign Sovereign, State, or Power, with Slaves, by or on Account of any of His Majesty's Subjects, or by Means of their Ships, Capital, or Credit; and to prevent the fitting out of Foreign Slave Ships from British Ports: — Preamble.

And whereas His MAJESTY, by His Order in Council, bearing Date the fifteenth day of August, one thousand eight hundred and five, was pleased to order, " That it should not be lawful, except by special " Licence as therein mentioned, for any Slave or Slaves to be landed upon " any of the Coasts, or imported or brought into any of the Ports, Har- " bours, Creeks, or Roads, or within the Limits, Jurisdictions, and Terri- " tories of any of the Settlements, Islands, Colonies, or Plantations on the " Continent of *America* or in the *West Indies*, which have been surren- " dered to His Majesty's Arms during the present War, until further Order, " upon pain, that all Slaves so landed or brought contrary to the true " Intent and Meaning of that Order, together with the Vessels bringing in " the same, or from which the same should be landed, and their Cargoes, " should become forfeited to His Majesty, His Heirs and Successors; but the — Recital of Order in Council.

124.

A

W illiam Wilberforce left another important legacy — one that is not nearly as well known about the life of this great Christian statesman. Indeed, while Wilberforce was mightily used to abolish the heinous slave trade — and (while on his deathbed) saw the culmination of a decades-long effort to abolish slavery itself throughout the British Empire — there was more to this unique man's life.

What is not well known is that Wilberforce's belief in the authority of the Bible, which gave him much of his motivation to rid the Empire of particular evils, was a legacy that he passed on to his son, who, in turn, wanted to improve British society. His son, of course, had a ready example to follow as he tackled a blight that was to affect his nation: the adverse social impact of Darwinian thinking.

It is well known in England that Samuel Wilberforce, the bishop of Oxford, was the creationist who engaged in a public debate with Thomas Huxley over Darwin's just-released *On the Origin of the Species*. As legend has it, evolutionist Huxley won the 1860 debate, just as it is the common myth today that William Jennings Bryan was a

Samuel Wilberforce

total failure at the famous 1925 Scopes monkey trial in Tennessee (in which Bryan also defended the Bible's account of origins). Both legends are largely inaccurate and bear only some semblance to what actually happened. The American and British publics, however, remain largely unaware of the truth of history.

Although Samuel was trained as a theologian and was a professor of theology at Oxford, he was also a professor of mathematics — and an amateur naturalist of some experience (who had studied Darwinian evolution in the months before his encounter with Huxley). Being knowledgeable in the sciences, Samuel had written a review of Darwin's book for the *Quarterly Review* (July 1860). In fact, when Darwin himself read the article, he commented that Wilberforce's review was "uncommonly clever; it picks out with skill all the most conjectural parts, and brings forward well all the difficulties."[1]

What is most recounted about the Oxford debate is the alleged exchange of Wilberforce supposedly turning to Huxley, and with a derisive smile, asking Huxley, "Was it through his grandfather or his grandmother that he [Huxley] descended from a monkey?" Some sources reported that Huxley supposedly quipped, "I would rather be descended from an ape than a bishop."

Historian J.R. Lucas has summarized what probably happened at the historic debate — and whether Wilberforce even made his monkey comment. In the *Historical Journal*[2] (and which was summarized in the journal *Nature*[3]), Lucas states that Wilberforce made "serious scientific arguments." This historian added that it was doubtful that Wilberforce ever asked Huxley whether he was descended from a monkey or ape. Also, Lucas says that Wilberforce was not inclined to be of the temperament to ridicule people anyway, contrary to what has become folklore.

Now, in the course of refuting evolution and man's supposed ancestry, Wilberforce probably did make some reference to monkeys or apes. In general, though, he concentrated on two general topics. First, that there was no evidence of new creatures forming that could be observed. Second, while natural selection might cause a creature to look different than its predecessors, that difference did not lead a creature to become a different one; he argued for fixity of creatures within their kind.[4]

As *The Athenaeum* observed, "The most eminent naturalists assembled at Oxford" took Wilberforce's side.[5] Furthermore, according to another source, Huxley was not convincing in his attempts to counter Wilberforce's arguments.[6]

It is not surprising that Samuel, being sensitive to humanitarian matters due to his special upbringing, saw

the possible racist consequences of Darwin's new model of origins. Darwin posited the racist belief that some people groups were more advanced in their evolution than others.

There is another legacy to note in relation to both Wilberforces and their Christian faith, but it is an unfortunate one. The denomination in which both were so active no longer stands up for the accuracy and authority of the Bible. While Samuel defended the Genesis account of creation in his famous debate with Huxley, the Church of England eventually decided that evolution could be embraced. Both father and son would be shocked beyond belief at this compromise today.

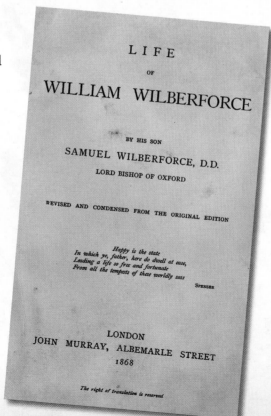

LIFE
OF
WILLIAM WILBERFORCE

BY HIS SON
SAMUEL WILBERFORCE, D.D.
LORD BISHOP OF OXFORD

REVISED AND CONDENSED FROM THE ORIGINAL EDITION

Happy is the state
In which ye, father, here do dwell at ease,
Leading a life so free and fortunate
From all the tempests of these worldly seas
SPENSER

LONDON
JOHN MURRAY, ALBEMARLE STREET
1868

The right of translation is reserved

Editors Note:
Mark Looy wrote his master's thesis (1983) on William Wilberforce. His 25-year study of this extraordinary man has taken him to research libraries throughout the United States and England (including a visit to Wilberforce's home in Hull, England). The co-founder of the Answers in Genesis ministry (builders of the large Creation Museum near Cincinnati, OH), Mark has been an avid student and historian of the creation/evolution controversy for more than 35 years.

[1] Charles Darwin, *Life and Letters*, Vol. 2, Francis Darwin, ed. (New York: Appleton and Co., 1911), p. 117–118.
[2] R. Lucas, "Wilberforce and Huxley: A Legendary Encounter," *The Historical Journal*, 22:313–330, 1979.
[3] J.R. Lucas, "Wilberforce No Ape," *Nature*, 287:480 (October 9, 1980).
[4] For a refutation of natural selection as a mechanism to change one animal to another, visit www.AnswersInGenesis.org.
[5] See G.S. Carter, *A Hundred Years of Evolution* (London: Sidgewick and Jackson, 1957), p. 70.
[6] William Tuckwell, *Reminiscences of Oxford* (London: Cassell and Company, 1900), p. 52.

When William Wilberforce turned his life over to Jesus Christ at the age of 25, he was transformed to such a great and marvelous degree by God's grace that he was called and used by God, along with his associates, to help initiate the transformation of Great Britain and to witness the Second Great Awakening revival in the process. A little man beset by severe health problems, he understood clearly that he lived and moved and had his being only in the resurrection power of Jesus Christ. Thus, he writes to all of us to join him in the glorious grace and love of God so we too can be instruments of God's grace:

> But the nature of the holiness to which the desires of the true Christian are directed, is no other than the restoration of the image of God; and as to the manner of acquiring it, disclaiming with indignation every idea of attaining it by his own strength, all his hopes of possessing it rest altogether on the divine assurances of the operation of the Holy Spirit in those who cordially embrace the Gospel of Christ. He knows therefore that this holiness is not to *precede* his reconciliation to God, and be its *cause*; but to *follow* it, and be its *effect*. That, in short, it is by *faith in Christ* only that he is to be justified in the sight of God; to be delivered from the condition of a child of wrath and a slave of Satan; to be adopted into the family of God; to become an heir of God and a joint heir with Christ, entitled to all the privileges which belong to this high relation; here, to the Spirit of grace, and a partial renewal after the image of his Creator; hereafter, to the more perfect possession of the Divine likeness, and an inheritance of eternal glory.[1]

This is great news every Christian should rejoice in. Wilberforce goes on to remind us that without the redemption of Christ we are only sinners:

> Of sinners, on the other hand, it is declared that they are of their "father the devil"; while on earth, they are styled "his children," "his servants"; they are said "to do his works," to be "subjects of his kingdom": at length "they shall partake his portion," when the merciful Savior shall be changed into an avenging Judge, and shall pronounce that dreadful sentence, "Depart from me, ye cursed, into everlasting fire, prepared for the devil and his angels."[2]

Christ's deliverance from our state of sinfulness turns us into new men and women:

> But the Christian's is a far different temper: not a temper of sordid sensuality, or lazy apathy, or dogmatizing pride, or disappointed ambition: more truly independent of worldly estimation than philosophy with all her boasts, it forms a perfect contrast to epicurean selfishness, to stoical pride, and to cynical brutality. It is a temper compounded of firmness, and complacency, and peace, and love; manifesting itself in acts of kindness and of courtesy; a kindness not pretended, but genuine; a courtesy not false and

superficial, but cordial and sincere. In the hour of popularity it is not intoxicated or insolent; in the hour of unpopularity it is not desponding or morose; unshaken in constancy, unwearied in benevolence, firm without roughness, and assiduous without servility.[3]

Wilberforce contrasts the person who possesses this redeemed nature with the miserable nature of nominal Christians:

> [There is] a vast difference between the habitual temper of his mind, and that of the generality of nominal Christians, who are almost entirely taken up with the concerns of the present world.[4]

Wilberforce diagnoses what he calls "the grand radical defect in the practical system of these nominal Christians" as:

> their forgetfulness of all the peculiar doctrines of the religion which they profess — the corruption of human nature; the atonement of the Savior; and the sanctifying influence of the Holy Spirit.[5]

Wilberforce portrait

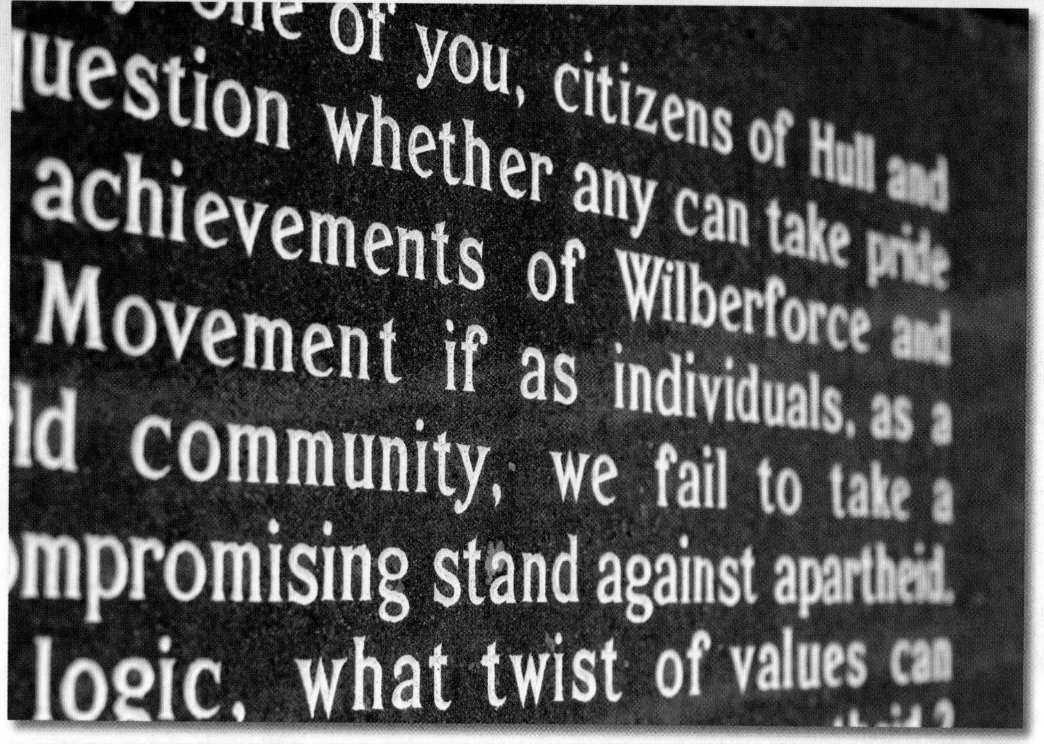

Declaration against slavery, Wilberforce House Museum and Nelson Mandela Gardens, Kingston-upon-Hull, East Yorkshire

On the other hand, for the person who has truly accepted Jesus Christ as his or her Lord and Savior:

> . . . the example of Christ is their pattern, the word of God is their rule; there they read, that "without holiness no man shall see the Lord." It is the description of real Christians, that they are gradually "changed into the image of their Divine Master. . . ."
>
> It is not merely, however, the fear of misery, and the desire of happiness, by which they are actuated in their endeavors to excel in all holiness; they love it for its own sake. . . . This determination has its foundations indeed in a deep and humiliating sense of his exalted majesty and infinite power, and of their own extreme inferiority and littleness, attended with a settled conviction of its being their duty as his creatures, to submit in all things to the will of their great Creator. But these awful impressions are relieved and ennobled by an admiring sense of the infinite perfections and infinite amiableness of the Divine character; animated by a confiding though humble hope of his fatherly kindness and protection, and quickened by the grateful recollection of immense and continually increasing obligations. This is the Christian love of God! A love compounded of admiration, of preference, of hope, of trust, of joy; chastised by reverential awe, and wakeful with continual gratitude.[6]

Finally, William Wilberforce tells us clearly that there is salvation in no one else but Jesus Christ:

> Let us then, each for himself, solemnly ask ourselves, whether *we* have fled for refuge to the appointed hope? And whether *we* are habitually looking to it, as to the only source of consolation? "Other foundation can no man lay": there is no other ground of dependence, no other plea for pardon; but here there is hope, even to the uttermost. Let us labor then to affect our hearts with a deep conviction of our need of a Redeemer, and of the value of His offered mediation. Let us fall down humbly before the throne of God, imploring

pity and pardon in the name of the Son of His love. Let us beseech Him to give us a true spirit of repentance, and of hearty undivided faith in the Lord Jesus. Let us not be satisfied till the cordiality of our belief be confirmed to us by that character of the apostle, "that to as many as believe Christ is precious"; and let us strive to increase daily in love towards our blessed Savior; and pray earnestly that "we may be filled with joy and peace in believing, that we may abound in hope, through the power of the Holy Ghost." Let us diligently put in practice the directions formerly given for cherishing and cultivating the principles of the love of Christ. With this view let us labor assiduously to increase in knowledge, that ours may be a deeply rooted and rational affection. By frequent meditation on the incidents of our Savior's life, and still more on the astonishing circumstances of His death; by often calling to mind the state from which He proposes to rescue us, and the glories of His heavenly kingdom; by continual intercourse with Him of prayer and praise, of dependence and confidence in dangers, of hope and joy in our brighter hours; let us endeavor to keep Him constantly present to our minds, and to render all our conceptions of Him more distinct, lively, and intelligent. The title of Christian is a reproach to us if we estrange ourselves from Him after whom we are denominated. The name of Jesus is not to be to us like the Allah of the Mohammedans, a talisman or an amulet to be worn on the arm, as an external badge merely,

"In the language of Scripture, Christianity is not a geographical, but a moral term. It is not the being a native of a Christian country: it is a condition, a state; the possession of a peculiar nature, with the qualities and properties which belong to it."
– William Wilberforce

and symbol of our profession, and to preserve us from evil by some mysterious and unintelligible potency; but it is to be engraven deeply on the heart, there written by the finger of God himself in everlasting characters. It is our title known and understood to present peace and future glory. The assurance which it conveys of a bright reversion, will lighten the burdens and alleviate the sorrows of life; and in some happier moments it will impart to us somewhat of that fullness of joy which is at God's right hand, enabling us to join even here in the heavenly hosanna, "Worthy is the Lamb that was slain to receive power, and riches, and wisdom, and strength, and honor, and glory, and blessing. . . . Blessing, and honor, and glory, and power, be unto him that sitteth upon the throne, and unto the Lamb, for ever and ever" (Rev. 5: 12–13).[7]

In an age of watered-down Christianity, in an age of nominal Christians, these powerful God-ordained words of William Wilberforce lit a spark that changed the world. The change was all the more awesome not because it stopped the ancient and lucrative trade in human beings created in the image of God (for it did that), nor because it reformed the child labor laws, protected women, and improved the living conditions of millions (for these words did all that), but because it brought people to the saving knowledge of Jesus Christ so that they were transformed into new creations who were liberated from sin and death into the glorious freedom and light of the kingdom of God Almighty.

If we understand and take his words to heart, then we too will be more than conquerors in Jesus Christ! And so, with this transforming knowledge, we will go forth into all the world proclaiming liberation for the millions of people who are captive to sin and death.

The essence of this power is God's grace, as William Wilberforce summarized so eloquently:

THAT God so loved the world, as of his tender mercy to give his only Son Jesus Christ for our redemption:

That our blessed Lord willingly left the glory of the Father, and was made man:

That "he was despised and rejected of men; a man of sorrows, and acquainted with grief":

That "he was wounded for our transgressions"; and "was bruised for our iniquities":

That "the Lord laid on him the iniquity of us all":

That at length he humbled himself even to the death of the cross, for us, miserable sinners; to the end that all who, with hearty repentance and true faith should come to him, might not perish, but have everlasting life:

That he is now at the right hand of God, making intercession for his people:

That, "being reconciled to God by the death of his Son, we may come boldly unto the throne of grace, to obtain mercy and find grace to help in time of need":

That our Heavenly Father "will surely give his Holy Spirit to them that ask him":

That "the Spirit of God must dwell in us" and that "if any man hath not the Spirit of Christ, he is none of his."

That by this Divine influence "we are to be renewed in knowledge after the image of Him who created us," and "to be filled with the fruits of righteousness, to the praise of the glory of his grace"; that, "being thus made meet for the

inheritance of the saints in light," we shall sleep in the Lord; and that, when the last trumpet shall sound, this corruption shall put on incorruption; and that, being at length perfected after his likeness, we shall be admitted into his heavenly kingdom.[8]

If you are as excited by these words as we are, if you want to be part of God's plan to change the world, then be encouraged by seeing the movie *Amazing Grace* and reading William Wilberforce's book *A Practical View of the Prevailing Religious System of Professed Christians in the Higher and Middle Classes of this Country Contrasted with Real Christianity*.[9] Our friend Bob Beltz has edited a wonderful modern translation of William Wilberforce's book called: *William Wilberforce's Real Christianity*.

Finally, if you are transformed by God's grace by humbly accepting His salvation through Jesus Christ alone, then listen to the words of God himself concerning His call to you at His resurrection:

And as they were saying these things, He Himself stood among them. He said to them, "Peace to you!" But they were startled and terrified and thought they were seeing a ghost. "Why are you troubled?" He asked them. "And why do doubts arise in your hearts? Look at My hands and My feet, that it is I Myself! Touch Me and see, because a ghost does not have flesh and bones as you can see I have." Having said this, He showed them His hands and feet. But while they still could not believe because of [their] joy and were amazed, He asked them, "Do you have anything here to eat?" So they gave Him a piece of a broiled fish, and He took it and ate in their presence.

Then He told them, "These are My words that I spoke to you while I was still with you — that everything written about Me in the Law of Moses, the Prophets, and the Psalms must be fulfilled." Then He opened their minds to understand the Scriptures. He also said to them, "This is what is written: the Messiah would suffer and rise from the dead the third day, and repentance for forgiveness of sins would be proclaimed in His name to all the nations, beginning at Jerusalem. You are witnesses of these things. And look, I am sending you what My Father promised. As for you, stay in the city until you are empowered from on high" (Luke 24:36–49; HCSB).

"But you will receive power when the Holy Spirit has come upon you, and you will be My witnesses in Jerusalem, in all Judea and Samaria, and to the ends of the earth" (Acts 1:8; HCSB).

1   William Wilberforce, *A Practical View of the Prevailing Religious System of Professed Christians in the Higher and Middle Classes of this Country Contrasted with Real Christianity* (London: T. Cadell, jun. & W. Davies, 1797), p. 166.
2   Ibid., p. 150.
3   Ibid., p. 126.
4   Ibid., p. 101.
5   Ibid., p. 162–163.
6   Ibid., p. 82.
7   Ibid., p. 70–71.
8   Ibid., p. 34–35.
9   William Wilberforce, *A Practical View of the Prevailing Religious System of Professed Christians in the Higher and Middle Classes of this Country Contrasted with Real Christianity* (London: T. Cadell, jun. & W. Davies, 1797).

Wilberforce Statue

When William Wilberforce died on July 29, 1833, Parliament resolved that he should be buried in Westminster Abbey. His grave is next to his friend, William Pitt the Younger, in the north transept. In 1840, a statue by Samuel Joseph was set up in the north choir aisle. The inscription on the statue reads:

To the memory of William Wilberforce (born in Hull, August 24th, 1759, died in London, July 29th, 1833) for nearly half a century a member of the House of Commons, and, for six Parliaments during that period, one of the two representatives for Yorkshire. In an age and country fertile in great and good men, he was among the foremost of those who fixed the character of their times; because to high and various talents, to warm benevolence, and to universal candour, he added the abiding eloquence of a Christian life. Eminent as he was in every department of public labour, and a leader in every work of charity, whether to relieve the temporal or the spiritual wants of his fellow-men, his name will ever be specially identified with those exertions which, by the blessing of God, removed from England the guilt of the African slave trade, and prepared the way for the abolition of slavery in every colony of the Empire: in the prosecution of these objects he relied, not in vain, on God; but in the progress he was called to endure great obloquy and great opposition: he outlived, however, all emnity; and in the evening of his days, withdrew from public life and public observation to the bosom of his family. Yet he died not

Statue of William Wilberforce in Westminster Abbey

Tribute to William Wilberforce

(on the plaque in Westminster Abbey where he is buried)

In an age and country fertile in great and good men,
He was among the foremost of those who fixed the character of our times
because to high and various talents, to warm benevolence, and to universal candour.
He added the abiding eloquence of the Christian life.
Eminent as he was in every department of public labour
And a leader in every work of charity.

Whether to relive the temporal or the spiritual wants of his fellow men
His name will ever be specially identified with those exertions
Which, by the blessing of God, removed from England
The guilt of the African slave trade,
and prepared the way for the Abolition of Slavery
in every colony of the Empire.

unnoticed or forgotten by his country: the peers and
commons of England, with the lord chancellor and
the speaker at their head, in solemn procession
from their respective houses, carried him
to his fitting place among the mighty
dead around, here to repose: till, through
the merits of Jesus Christ, his only
Redeemer and Saviour (whom, in his
life and in his writings he had desired to
glorify), he shall rise in the resurrection
of the just.

William Pitt is buried next to Wilberforce.

THIS MONUMENT
IS ERECTED BY PARLIAMENT,
TO WILLIAM PITT,
SON OF WILLIAM, EARL OF CHATHAM,
IN TESTIMONY OF GRATITUDE
FOR THE EMINENT PUBLIC SERVICES,
AND OF REGRET FOR THE IRREPARABLE LOSS
OF THAT GREAT AND DISINTERESTED MINISTER

In conjunction with the film, *Amazing Grace*, Bristol Bay Productions and Walden Media have launched a campaign to abolish modern day slavery. To learn more about slavery and to become an advocate by signing the petition at their website:

theamazingchange.com

To go deeper and for more great articles, insights, information, and reflections by some of the best William Wilberforce scholars, please go to www.movieguide.org. With proof of purchase of *The Amazing Grace of Freedom*, you will be able to access more great articles and insights into William Wilberforce.

For more information, call or write:
MOVIEGUIDE®
2510-G Las Posas Rd.
Camarillo, CA 93010
805-383-2000 tel.
805-383-4089 fax
www.movieguide.org
(800) 899-6684

Photo Credits:

Alamy 28, 39, 50, 53, 64, 130, 136, 138
Ariadne Van Zandbergen 27
Bryan Miller 109
Corbis 43, 58, 60
Getty 31, 33, 71, 120, 128, 134
Superstock 115

KEN WALES

is a veteran filmmaker whose credits include being the Producer of feature films *Amazing Grace: The Story of William Wilberforce; The Tamarind Seed* (Julie Andrews, Omar Shariff); *Wild Rovers* (William Holden, Ryan O'Neal), and for Billy Graham, *The Prodigal*. Wales also Line Produced/Associate Produced *Darling Lili* (Julie Andrews, Rock Hudson); *Islands in the Stream* (George C. Scott); and *The Party* and *Revenge of the Pink Panther*, both starring Peter Sellers.

On network television Wales was Executive Producer for the critically acclaimed CBS series *Christy*, and won a Golden Globe and Emmy nomination as Co-Producer of the ABC miniseries *John Steinbeck's East of Eden*.

He is also the author of the WW II historical novel *Sea of Glory*, which he is preparing to film.

SUSAN WALES,

is a television producer, speaker, and author of numerous books including, *Faith in Gods and Generals*. A novelist, she is also the co-author of a series political thrillers, *The Chase, The Replacement*, and *The Candidate*. Best known for her *Match Made in Heaven* series and for her gift books, she co-wrote the *Keepsakes* series with author Alice Gray. Other publishing credits include columns and contributing articles to women's magazines and periodicals. She is the Executive Producer of the Annual MOVIEGUIDE® Awards presented to family films with redemptive values on PAX-TV. She is also a board member of the Parents Television Council, and co-produced a fundraiser for the UCLA Family Development Center. She and her husband, producer Ken Wales, live in Pacific Palisades, California. They have a daughter Megan and a granddaughter, Hailey Elizabeth.

TED BAEHR,

founder and Publisher of MOVIEGUIDE® and Chairman of The Christian Film & Television Commission, is a well-known movie critic, educator, lecturer, and media pundit. He has written numerous books, including *Culture-Wise Family* (Regal) and *Getting the Word Out* (Harper & Row). Dr. Baehr was president of the organization that produced *The Chronicles of Narnia: The Lion, the Witch and the Wardrobe*, boasting 37 million viewers and winning an Emmy Award. Dr. Baehr also produced hundreds of programs for PBS television. Dr. Baehr is on the board of many organizations, and has been a featured guest on programs such as: Oprah, Hannity and Colmes, CNN, ABC, Fox News, MSNBC, and Entertainment Tonight.

Meet the Authors

Also Available . . .

A JOURNEY THROUGH THE LIFE OF
William Wilberforce
the abolitionist who changed the face of a nation

by **KEVIN BELMONTE**

Leading Wilberforce scholar and consultant for the movie "Amazing Grace"

- Comprehensive historical overview — perfect for students ages 12 and up
- Dr. Kevin Belmonte, one of the world's leading scholars dedicated to educating the public about William Wilberforce

Walk the fascinating pathways and historic halls of England as you retrace the steps of legendary abolitionist and staunch Christian man of faith William Wilberforce. This full-color, unique guide to Wilberforce's life is a great tool for anyone interested in the life of this amazing man. It includes descriptions of his work on behalf of social justice issues like slavery and the end of poverty, as well as his many achievements, portraits of him and his contemporaries, and photographs of historic sites in England. Intended for a general audience, this fascinating book is great for anyone wanting to learn more about this man known as "the friend of humanity."

ISBN 13: 978-0-89221-671-0
Four Color • 128 pages • Casebound 5 x 8 • Retail: $14.99

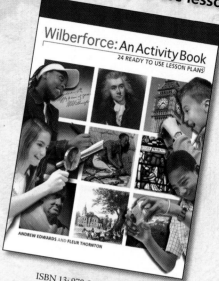

Wilberforce: An Activity Book
24 READY TO USE LESSON PLANS

ANDREW EDWARDS AND FLEUR THORNTON

ISBN 13: 978-0-89221-672-7
32 pages • Paper • 8 ½ x 11 • Retail: $6.99

Sample Spreads from A Journey Through the Life of William Wilberforce

The Slaves' Champion: The Life, Deeds, and Historical Days of William Wilberforce, first published in London in 1861, is an accurate and historical biography of the amazing abolitionist, William Wilberforce. Published soon after his death, this book is a revealing look into his way of life, his impact on society, his Christian character and beliefs, and the fascinating customs and culture of the era. The book includes:

- Reflections of those who knew him
- Correspondence from Wilberforce to his friends and colleagues
- Historical facts and perspective on his accomplishments
- Faithfully reproduced from the vintage original

ISBN 13: 978-0-89221-670-3 • 240 pages • Paper • 5 x 8
Special Retail price $7.99 ($12.00 Value)

Available at Christian Bookstores Nationwide